SURVIVING SITUATIONS

Finding Courage To Succeed In Spite of Life's Painful Moments

TIESHENA DAVIS

Purposely Created
PUBLISHING GROUP

Surviving Shocking Situations

Copyright © 2013 Tieshena Davis

Unless otherwise indicated, scripture quotations are from the New King James Version®. Copyright © 1982 by Thomas Nelson, Inc. All rights reserved.

Published by: Purposely Created Publishing Group™
Editor: Trelani Duncan

Printed in the United States of America

ISBN: 0-615-91309-1
ISBN-13: 978-0-615-91309-4

Special discounts are available on bulk quantity purchases by book clubs, associations and special interest groups. For details email: Hello@PurposelyCreatedPG.com or call (866) 674-3340.

For more information, log onto
www.PurposelyCreatedPG.com

Dedication

In loving memory of my:
Great-Grandmother, Ernestine "Tiny" Lee
Best Friend, Bonita Young
Uncle Linden Smith, Jr.

Each day, the rays of your light continue to guide,
protect and encourage me.

Your spirit has helped move mountains.

I will always love you!

To all of the victorious women, who once was a young girl,
lost in a cold world; this is for you, sis!

Table of Contents

Acknowledgments

First and foremost, I give thanks to God for being the source of my strength, my provider and protector.

To my daughter, Siva – You're my #1 motivator. Each day I live for YOU.

To my fiancé, Corey Reid – Thank you for believing in me, encouraging me to take risks and helping me to discover my life's purpose. I love you!

To my best friend, Kavara McDonald – I don't think there is a word to express the amount of gratitude that I have for all of the support you have given me. I'm utterly blessed to have a friend like you.

To my dad, Harold Smith – Thank you for illustrating perseverance. You're my living legend!

To my earth angels, the four women who unconditionally opened up their homes, wallets, arms, ears and hearts to me when times were rough: Brenda Young, Cherisse Woodson, Mary Price, and Monita Short-Ellis – Thank you for giving me the opportunity to *feel* what it's like to be a daughter of a wonderful mother.

To my village, Aunt Lynn, Aunt Tara, Aunt Val and Nucci – It's the simplest things you say that motivate me to strive for my very best. Your words are constantly with me!

To my mentor, Katrina M. Harrell – Thank you for selflessly taking me under your wing and helping me stay purposely-driven. You're a rare gem that I'm fortunate to have!

To Lucinda Cross – I thank God for our divine connection. Thanks for lending me some power!

To my amazing co-authors – Thank you for investing in my vision with your gift of writing and compassion to empower others. I will always and FOREVER be grateful for your trust, honesty, contribution, and support.

To my #CEODivas: Jessica Grace White, Mary Taylor, Quinn Conyers, Sharmetra Pittman, Jaemellah Kemp, S.Monique Smith, Lisa Fleet and Shona Barnes – Each of you are the *epitome* of a true role model. Our young women need to see more faces like yours on TV. Thanks for your continuous support!

To all of my friends and family, past radio show guests, my listeners and social media followers.

– You're my inspiration

Foreword

By Lucinda Cross

COURAGE is the common denominator!

Can COURAGE be bought? Yep! Absolutely! You just bought fourteen stories worth, or at least you've taken the first step towards your survival and getting stronger. This book is what I call an "on-time word."

As I humbly endorse this book that helps you chart the course for your own strength, I enthusiastically said yes when asked to write this foreword. This is an invaluable resource worthy of diligent and strategic application.

I have spent the majority of my entrepreneurial journey focused on transitions and transformations. I work very hard to be successful in my own life, but also to help push other people to become successful in their lives.

In my journey, I remind people to *feast on faith and fast on fear*. I encountered one of the most difficult challenges life could have given me. The loss of my mother in May 2013, the weekend of Mother's Day, was the most shocking and tragic situation for me. Courage is the only thing that keeps me seeking God, trusting God, and loving God through hurt and pain. Suddenly she was here and suddenly she left. Her legacy is COURAGE, strength, and tenacity. As you read this book, think of your own legacy of courage and what it breeds. My purpose has been birthed out of shocking situations and overcoming painful life lessons. I encourage you to open up your eyes and your heart, and really let the stories in this book sink in.

I believe that when you open up to fully absorb a small portion of the COURAGE imparted from each author in this book who lovingly shared their story, it won't be long before you'll find the courage you've been looking for to move forward and do what God has called you to do.

As you read *Surviving Shocking Situations,* you will realize this book is based on loving instead of hating, forgiving instead of anger, healing together instead of suffering alone. This book is about staying open to new ideas and making better decisions. It's a message of victory and overcoming. That is what most of us are looking for in life. We want the truth, the deep experience of being strong in our weakest moments.

While most books offer advice from the outside, *Surviving Shocking Situation* is about finding the COURAGE from within where it really counts. In these pages, you'll find the importance of digging deeper, regardless of your external circumstances.

If you are reading this foreword before purchasing this book, here are three very good reasons to buy now:

1. First, the stories and life lessons are true testaments of success after enduring various shocking situations. These stories were strategically chosen just for you to reference when life throws you a curve ball.

2. Second, applying what you will learn from other's life lessons will allow you to look at your own life and assess what is working for you and what is not working for you. The lessons will save you years of suffering and stagnation.

3. Third, it's a bargain! The author should have priced this book at its true value of at least $100. Yes, $100 or more. The stories are priceless and the experiences that each author encountered and shared in this book are priceless.

If you already purchased this book, make sure you have your pen and notepad ready to take notes. Jot down any "ah ha" moments, and keep tissues nearby as you are emotionally and spiritually cleansed.

It's your time, Ms. Courageous to walk the yellow brick road to get YOU back.

- Get your love back
- Get your life back
- Get your power back
- Get your truth back
- Get your strength back
- Get your COURAGE back!

You have just invested in a buffet of COURAGE; eat up and gift someone else with a copy.

Thank you for allowing me to be a part of your vision, Tieshena Davis. You are an angel, a COURAGEous woman of valor!

Lucinda Cross

Author of *Corporate Mom Dropouts* and
The Road to Redemption

Introduction

At approximately 8:50 am on Friday, October 11, 2013, right after posting an inspirational message on my Facebook page, God whispered in my ear, *"You are bent, yet not broken."* Then he told me not to delay on delivering this message to the women that needed to hear it. For a moment, I was slightly alarmed and overwhelmed by what he assigned me to do. But I quickly realized that time is of the essence and there was a woman out there suffering in silence and ready to die—literally and figuratively.

It took no longer than 10 minutes to think about how little ole me was going to deliver this message to the masses. Then another whisper, *"Do a book collaboration with other women who have experienced painful, shocking situations, but turned tragedy into triumph."* I began to get a warm sensation in my chest, my arms began to shiver, and I began to cry and smile uncontrollably. I texted my mentor and called my fiancé to tell them what I was experiencing. Both told me to take action swiftly. Immediately, I wrote down fifteen names of the women I wanted to be a part of the project, or more so, mission. I bombarded them with text messages, phone calls, Facebook messages, and emails explaining the vision and each of them said *Yes, let's do it.*

Now the vision has been fully manifested in this book. A compilation of candid stories from women who have endured the most unthinkable and unimaginable circumstances in life, but used their experiences to successfully overcome adversity. Each of our stories will empower you to *seek* and *embrace* true success achieved through **Courage**, **Liberation, Resilience,** and **Victory**.

If you've ever asked yourself these questions or know someone who is currently in this state of mind, this book should be *read thoroughly* and *referenced often* to answer questions such as:

- How do I find the courage to move beyond layers of pain and suffering?

- What should I do, who should I call, and where do I go when life has simply broken my heart?

- What are positive alternatives to giving up when I don't see a way out of shock, hurt or pain?

- How do I discover my purpose, voice or true identity?

This book will provoke you to build the courage needed for you to SURVIVE and THRIVE, above and beyond your obstacles.

We challenge you to **Embrace The Process!**

TIESHENA DAVIS

Existing With No Identity

"Father, Forgive Them, For They Know Not What They Do." – Luke 23:34

Being born into a world of abandonment not only paralyzes your will to live, but fuels your will to succeed. For years, not knowing what true security felt like scarred me in a way that only a homeless ambitionist can comprehend. Many times, I've wondered, "Why did this happen to me? What did I do wrong? Where will I be? Who loves me? How am I going to make it?" What I've realized is that many questions will remain unanswered until you learn to *stop wondering* and begin to *start seeking* the truth. Every unfortunate experience of pain in my life has led me to seek the higher purpose of my existence. It wasn't until recently that I discovered how my adversities became a cornerstone of my redemption and triumph.

This is my story, one of a woman who was birthed into a generational stronghold of abandonment and fear, but later found the courage to discover her true identity, inner power and life's purpose.

I was born in Philadelphia, Pennsylvania in 1981 during the emerging era of crack cocaine. Unbeknownst to me, the drug epidemic and its tangible disease would involuntarily become a part of my life history. The influence it had on my parents forced me to deal with many unfair decisions, difficulties and memories. As I think back, I recall encountering my first difficult defining moment in life around the age of six years old. I remember my aunt walking through the living room into the kitchen yelling, "Tiny, Grandmom, where are you?!" That call left me confused and disturbed as I began to think to myself, "Why is she calling her Grandmom? If that's my mom, how is she my aunt's grandmother?" Confusing right? These thoughts would often linger as I heard my other aunts, uncles and even my dad calling the woman I knew to be my mother "Grandmom."

At some point, I suddenly became frustrated, upset and hurt at not being able to solve this mystery. I would go to school and hear everyone talk about their mothers and in the back of my mind, say to myself, "I know she isn't my mom. She's my Grandmom, but where is my real mom?" Feelings of being ignored, unwanted and unworthy were deeply embedded in me at an early age, which eventually led me to becoming an incorrigible child who was very rebellious, and later hopeless during my teenage years. No one ever knew my feelings or concerns; they didn't bother to ask. Everyone assumed that I was okay because I had enough people in my life to fill the void that stemmed from my estranged mother. Although I had plenty of family and was highly loved, it didn't equate to the love that I longed for from my mother.

Around the age of eight, I started putting the pieces of the puzzle together to form a clear understanding of who my real mother was. I discovered that the person I was raised to call mommy was really my paternal great-grandmother, Ernestine "Tiny" Lee. Even with this information, I still felt confused and misled because I still didn't know who my real mother was, where she lived, or what caused her to abandon me.

Thankfully, one of my aunts and an older cousin took a brave move to reveal what had haunted me for years. One night, they sat me down in my aunt's bedroom to ask me if I wanted to know who my mom was. Filled with joy and excitement, I impulsively said yes, but suddenly felt knots in my stomach as I grabbed my aunt's hand to hear the words she was about to speak. She began to tell me my mother's name and that she left and moved to Baltimore, Maryland when I was an infant. Apparently, my mother was raised by an elderly woman in a group home with two other teenage girls and several teenage boys. From what I've been told, my mother was a very pretty, young girl. She was light-skinned, smart, and nicely proportioned.

She was also known as being fast, promiscuous and disobedient. She got pregnant and delivered me at the age of sixteen. When I was an infant, around one year of age, she left me at a friend's house unattended, and I was molested by an older man. When I was found, there was blood everywhere, and I was screaming at the top of my lungs. I was rushed to the hospital and the examination discovered that I had been sexually abused through the rectum. Wow, that was really hard to ponder! As a result of this incident, I was in and out of surgeries for the next ten years, and later told that I wouldn't be able to have children, depending on how my body developed.

My great-grandmother, Tiny, was my mom's teacher's aide and supposedly, one of her favorites. Tiny didn't know that my mom was pregnant by her oldest grandson, but when she found out, she immediately began to become more involved in my mom's life. She always made sure my mom ate a good meal each day and had the essentials needed while being pregnant and preparing for my arrival.

After the incident occurred, Tiny filed a police report and immediately filed for temporary custody of me. Although I was physically living with Tiny, she still allowed my mother to come visit me. While I was still an infant, the visitations suddenly stopped when my mother vanished and left with her mother from Baltimore who had also abandoned *her* as a child.

Soon after my second birthday, she returned to Philly and came to see me at Tiny's house. Somehow, in the midst of ongoing visitations, a level of trust was established and Tiny allowed her to take me out for the day without any supervision. My mom and maternal grandmother kidnapped me and took me to Baltimore. After a quick discovery of where I was, my great-grandfather, Blutey, searched the streets for my drug-addicted father to inform him of what happened. Immediately, Tiny, along with Blutey and my dad, rushed to Baltimore to bring me back to Philly.

That was the last presence of my mom. No more appearances, no letters, no pictures, no phone calls...nothing. Just everlasting painful thoughts of why, what, when, where, and how. Why did she leave me to get sexually abused? What was so important that she'd leave her baby alone? When is she coming back to get me? Where is she? How could she just disappear and move on as if I never existed?

Every time I'd think of her, I'd slowly gain self-hatred. I didn't know who I was. I started to question everyone and everything around me. At times, I even wondered if my father's family were really my blood relatives. I just felt like I was living in a huge fairytale, but it wasn't *Alice in Wonderland;* instead, it was *Tieshena's Nightmare on Haines Street.*

Just when you think a young child has endured enough pain and suffering, it gets worse. Yes, the only mother I knew, the one who never left me and always protected me suddenly leaves too, a few months after my eighth birthday.

For some reason, Tiny kept me home from school that day and yelled to me from sun up to sun down, *"Tieshena, find my heart pills!"* I'll never forget what that small, brown bottle and those tiny, white pills looked like. Usually, you couldn't miss them, but on this particular day, they just couldn't be found. When it was time to go to bed that night, she made one last request and asked me to look under the dresser for her pills. I knelt down, searched left to right, back and forth; still the bottle wasn't in sight. As I sat up to tell her that I didn't see the bottle, I looked to my right and saw her eyes rolling up to the sky, her body uncontrollably shaking, and white foam pouring from her mouth. Suddenly, she stopped shaking and stopped breathing. Just like that, in front of my face, Tiny passed away from a heart attack. The guilt I carried for years haunted me because I always thought it was my fault until I was old enough to learn about heart disease and death. With Tiny gone, my mother still absent and my father still consumed by his addiction, where would I go? This became the million-dollar question of my life.

"Tragedy is a tool for the living to gain wisdom, not a guide by which to live." - Robert Kennedy

Between the ages of nine and sixteen, I was moved around between four different houses with four different family members who each had different types of standards and expectations of me. At this point, I was a lost cause, or at least that's how I felt. I moved in with my paternal grandfather after Tiny passed away. Initially, it was the best feeling I ever had, but soon became the worst four years of my life. Everything that I did right was wrong, and everything that I did wrong I was abusively punished for. From fifth grade to eighth grade, I was *constantly* told that I wouldn't be "shit." I would live in the projects all of my life, I would be in the streets like my Dad, and I would be a failure. Aside from the occasional beatings from my grandfather and recovering dad, my punishments turned into being isolated in my room and given the silent treatment. Any time I'd try to break the ice by offering to do something around the house or cracking a joke about something that I saw in school, I was dismissed, shut down or ignored. After being treated like this for just about every week for at least four years straight, I became fed up. Here I was again, asking myself, "Why me?" and "Why did she leave me here with these people?" and "Is she ever coming back to get me?"

Enough was enough, it was either get away or take myself out of everyone else's way. I prayed every night for a miracle to happen so that I could be delivered from my misery. When God didn't answer soon enough, I began to ask him to just kill me. "Please, let me get hit by a stray bullet," "Please, let the house burn down," "Please, let me get hit by a car." When God didn't allow any of those things to happen, I started to become upset with Him too. I even gave up on Him by convincing myself that He didn't exist. In my eyes, He was just a myth. Suddenly, one of my prayers was answered and I was ready to conquer the world. I'd always see commercials about Job Corp and being able to attend all around the country. This was it! I just needed to hurry up and turn sixteen so that I could go.

Finally, my sixteenth birthday came. I spent the early part of my summer vacation hesitant to ask my grandfather if I could go because I knew how serious he was about school and getting an education. But I didn't have to worry much about his answer because he didn't want me back in his house anyway. So I asked, "Grandpop, will you take me downtown to sign up for Job Corp?" He answered yes. Honestly, I couldn't think of a better day in my sixteen years of being on earth at the time. I was ready to go, there was no turning back, and I REFUSED to ever be called a failure again. Nope, not on my watch. I wasn't going to be left behind again or end up on the streets like my dad. I was going to make it. I was going to be *the one* that exceeded and surpassed everyone's expectations. I was going to be *the one* who did it differently. Furthermore, I would be completely unapologetic for my ambition to succeed.

On September 2, 1997, I left Philly and arrived in Washington, DC ready to start a new life all by myself. There I was with my suitcase, an ounce of encouragement, a pound of uncertainty, and a *ton* of determination. Today, I am no longer hopeless, angry, filled with guilt or discouragement because of my past circumstances. I have a beautiful daughter, and my father is now sixteen years clean from his drug addiction and is actively in my life.

In the year 2000, at the age of nineteen, I finally met my mom and was able to get answers to a few of the questions that had been haunting me since I was a child. After meeting her for the first time, I had a life-changing epiphany that caused me to also meet *myself* for the very first time. I suddenly realized that all my life I was existing, but wasn't living. I had allowed the junk that I collected during my journey to totally consume my life and strip my identity. Each day, I worked, loved, laughed, cried, ate, yawned, slept, and breathed, but again, I wasn't living and I had no clue who I was. This realization was very alarming to me! Again, the question of "why me?" came back. Why was I given so much suffering to bear at such a young age?

> *"To live is to suffer, but to survive;*
> *well that's to find meaning in the suffering."* – DMX

Life Lesson: When life throws you a curveball, don't become a victim to your pain. Instead, seek the meaning in your suffering so you can discover new insights about your inner power and purpose.

Once I stopped *wondering* and began *seeking,* God revealed to me the reason for my pain and suffering. I learned that if I had not encountered those painful situations, I would not be qualified to do the work that He originated me to do. It all started to make sense; everything was preparation for my assignment as an adult. He was building my endurance to perform my purpose.

Now I can happily say I'm living in my destiny by helping others understand that they, too, can succeed in spite of their adversities in life. It was through deep self-conversation, self-evaluation and radical emotional acceptance that I discovered my purpose. You can too!

As I continue to travel on my journey in life, I'm constantly reminded of where I came from and how I've made it to this very moment. As crazy as it may sound, I'm utterly grateful for the adversity that I've endured. Without it, I would still be just existing!

"I wonder how many people I've look___   ___nd never se___ "

Have you all   ur true identit'

My beautiful   e
you to stop E.   1
life that wil.
Genuinely fall
offer.

*"There is no gr
honor your calli.
become most trul*

Don't let your ap   ___ars of the unknown alter your calling. it may look or feel impossible to overcome your situation, but you can do it. You have the power within you to prosper. Your visions, your dreams, and your happiness is a reality within reach. God has bestowed an everlasting protectant at the pit of your pain that will NOT allow any person, situation or circumstance to devour your power. Tap into it!

Begin your new life by committing to the following process of **C.H.A.N.G.E.**, and don't forget that God has your back, even at the cusp of your breakdown.

1. Check yourself.

Take a step back to evaluate YOU by asking yourself the hard questions and being receptive to honest answers. Take a thorough self-inventory of your strengths, weaknesses, needs, desires, beliefs, and fears. It may cut like a knife or leave a temporary bruise, but it will not kill you. It's through this process that you will begin to discover your true identity, purpose and inner power.

2. Honor your truth.

Build the courage to overcome your fear of knowing the truth, so you can begin to walk and live in a truthful life. God has already rolled out your red carpet; don't sacrifice your spiritual freedom in exchange for denial and self-pity. Pacifying the truth will only deteriorate your most precious commodities—your sanity, spirit and soul.

3. Activate your faith.

Having faith is not just about you. You must have faith in God, yourself, and other people to truly reap its rewards. When you are walking, believing, and living in faith, the world is much clearer because you are divinely connected with the power of understanding everything that happens in your journey. If you keep faith, you'll have no room for the junk, negativity, or insecurities. Your focus will be deeply rooted in becoming a better you and learning how to survive without a tangible substance. Faith is what nourishes you to survive. It does a body, soul, and mind good. *"For as the body without the spirit is dead, so faith without works is dead."* – James 2:26

4. Never give up.

There is a treasure buried in your troubles. You just have to go through the process of breakdown to get your breakthrough. Having the audacity to do whatever is necessary to make your most heartfelt desires manifest is not an option in the game of survival. When you feel like all odds are against you and there's no way to make it, ask yourself, "What do I have to lose if I'm already lost?" The answer is nothing; you have NOTHING to lose! You MUST stay determined to succeed in spite of the bumps, detours, and accidents along your journey.

5. Go beyond your limitations.

Challenge yourself each day to do something different. When negative thoughts begin to linger, open your mouth and speak the opposite of what you're thinking. Don't get distracted or discouraged by the things you can't control. Stay laser-focused on the things you can control and what you want to achieve.

6. Embrace change.

All things in life are subject to constant change and there are no guarantees on what may unfold. Even when you think you have it all figured out, life will surprise you. Invite the unknown and remain optimistic knowing that the only things to be discovered are the infinite possibilities.

Always keep in mind that any time you're in the midst of a breakthrough or transformation, you will also be in a battle of survival with the enemy. He is ready to sabotage your blessings in whatever way he can. He will try to attack your health (mental, emotional and physical), your finances, your relationships, and your perseverance. However, he can't block what's YOURS...Go get it!

About Tieshena

Described as a transformation catalyst, Tieshena Davis utilizes her personal stories of abandonment, courage and perseverance as tools to educate and empower her audiences. She believes that through sharing our stories we *heal, prepare* and *propel* for a new life that's full of possibilities and opportunities to thrive.

She is the founder and CEO of *Purposely Created Publishing Group*™ – a boutique publishing company committed to introducing literature that embodies empowerment via social awareness, education and personal transformation.

Additionally, Tieshena offers business management consulting services to help micro-entrepreneurs improve operational performance.

She is wholeheartedly committed and loves her profession, as it aligns with her divine calling; to help others discover their hidden potential, and to create success on their own terms.

To learn more, visit
www.ThriveWithTie.com

2

KATRINA M. HARRELL

Suffering In Silence:
Discovering My Voice After Being Voiceless

Whitney Houston has always been my favorite singer. I remember hearing her songs on the radio, watching her videos, stretching my underdeveloped six-year-old vocal chords to hit her notes. And in my mind, I did, every time. You couldn't tell me anything. I would be a famous singer when I grew up! I would be on stages and captivate crowds and little girls, just like me, all over the world. I was so convinced, I even wrote my own songs, sang in front of the mirror, and, according to my mother, I danced in front of her, showing off my latest moves. Like many little girls, I was naturally confident, untarnished by the world, and I just knew my voice would be heard someday until...

At six years old, my innocence, identity, and ultimately, my voice was taken from me by a person identified as a friend of my family who molested me multiple times—any chance he had. My small, trusting, innocent, and underdeveloped body was taken advantage of. Taking with it, my voice. For the next 25 years, I'd remain silent, suffering in that pain, going inward to a place where no one could violate me or my trust ever again.

As I'm writing this, I feel the resistance of addressing it; I feel like I'm giving this person power again. However, there is a knowingness in me that realizes I'm transferring that power stolen from me to you, a woman who's still suffering in silence and has no voice to stand up for herself.

I grew up in Washington, D.C. in the late '70s, '80s and '90s. My mom, a single mother, and I moved around a lot, so I attended many schools. She used to tell me stories of how I loved to dance and sing around the house before my voice was stolen. I'd say, "Hey, mommy, look at me!" and would go into a dancing fit like any typical three- four- or five year old would. Despite the dysfunction around me, the lack of stability, or the presence of my father on a consistent basis, I had the love and warmth of my loving, protective mother and her sisters and brothers, who loved me like I was their own. I knew who I was and, like any little girl, I used my voice. I knew there were issues in my life because my mom was always open with me, but I always felt protected. Through that feeling of protection, children learn to be who they are, trust who they are, and explore who they are. Feeling protected gives access to confidence.

Children are powerful indicators of character. They may not know how to articulate what they feel, but they know. I remember meeting *him* at a family dinner. I come from a loving family of aunts, uncles, and cousins who live by the motto, "A friend of a family member is automatically a friend of the family." We love people; we make friends and treat everyone like family. It's how we are and it's one of the things I love so much about us. So when *he* was introduced to us as a new friend at a family dinner, I didn't think anything of his presence. He sat quietly on the sofa and engaged in light, casual conversation with other family members. I remembered him because arrangements were made for my mom and I to stay with him. My mom was struggling at the time and needed a temporary place to stay. My family trusted him enough to allow us into his care. On the ride to his place, I remember feeling weird. He wasn't mean or rude, but the opposite actually. He bought me McDonald's and seemed to do whatever he could to win my trust. Though it worked, I still felt like something was weird about him. His choice of words, his comments, and the over-niceness didn't make me feel good. Ultimately, my intuition was correct.

It's important we listen to our children; they may not always know HOW to tell us, but they know. I later learned, as a mother, to allow my children to feel validated in their choices. If they don't feel comfortable giving Aunt so and so or Uncle such and such, or even Grandpa a hug and kiss, I do not force them to out of a false sense of what is polite and what isn't. Children have voices that deserve to be heard, validated and nurtured.

For several weeks (maybe even months), I was molested many times by this person. I can remember at least six times vividly. He always insisted that we take naps—he, my mom and I. I found it weird because my mom never made me take naps, but she followed. I'd sleep in the middle because I was small, and perhaps they were concerned I'd fall off the bed. One day while napping, my mom completely asleep, I felt this odd touch on my arm and hand. I tried to ignore it, but I felt it again; it persisted. Naturally, being six years old, I'd never seen or felt a penis before, so I had no idea what it was, but I knew it felt unfamiliar and weird. Then I heard a voice, "Here, put your hands on it." In my undeveloped mind, I suddenly realized what was happening. He was making me do something wrong. I knew it and my heart sped in fear. I was trying to decide whether I should wake my mom or scream, but then I remembered he showed us the gun he kept in a drawer near his bed. I also remembered overhearing him telling my mom a story about him taking advantage of a young girl in his past. I was scared he'd hurt me or my mom if I made a sound, so I remained quiet. I touched him and allowed him to touch me, violate me and force me to realize that suffering in silence was a reality I'd have to live with. I didn't utter a word for 25 years.

He was discovered. My mom found out what was going on, and when she did, we moved immediately. I'm not sure if he was arrested, but my parents proceeded with legal actions to have him jailed. I found out later that my family was so upset that one of my uncles allegedly wanted to have him murdered. The legal proceedings went on for a few weeks. I was a part of it, prepared by the court to testify.

Then suddenly, it all suddenly stopped. Nothing. He was never brought to justice and the subject was never mentioned again. I didn't utter another word about it for 25 years.

All pain is the same. The same incident can happen to two different girls and produce a different outcome. For some, they become abused again by other men in their lives or become promiscuous. For others, they lean toward the opposite of the spectrum; withdrawing inward, resisting their sexuality, becoming confused about it and often rejecting it because they don't understand how to embrace it. That was my story.

I found comfort going inward. Suddenly, all males were my enemy. They were not to be trusted, with the exception of my cousins, uncles, and dad. Other males were disgusting.

Middle school is when girls and boys really start noticing each other and dating. There may even be a few "fast" girls actually having sex. I couldn't understand why a girl would want to have sex. Boys, at the time, were gross. Even though I had crushes, I never wanted them to notice me. I was the complete opposite of the "fast" girls. While they wore their pain on their sleeves by being what we called "freaks" at that time, I was the opposite. I hid, not wanting anyone to notice me. I became withdrawn, stopped expressing myself, and stopped letting people know I existed. Because if they saw me, they would be able to hurt me. I couldn't trust people anymore; I couldn't trust my loved ones to protect me because I felt they hadn't. I had to learn to protect myself, build a wall, and cover myself in it. I felt if I stayed quiet and hidden, I would be safe.

I was the girl who wore baggy boy clothes, big glasses, and carried extra weight. I figured if I didn't look cute, boys wouldn't want me. Therefore, I couldn't be violated. But I developed fast. My hips and boobs developed early, and I hated it. I couldn't walk down the street as a typical preteen without some twenty to thirty-year-old man honking or gawking at me. I liked boys my age, but I was afraid of them. I remember in seventh grade, a popular boy was dared to kiss me. He ran up and kissed me and I ran out of the school lunch line, bursting into tears. To me, it felt like I was violated all over again. *My perception of myself and my inability to express my emotions impacted everything.* I had no voice. As a result, my relationships with men were impacted as a young, college-aged woman. I struggled, in some ways, to let people in and allow them to know Katrina.

I was suffering in silence. I didn't want to let people know what was going on with me. I figured if I just remained a 'good girl', did everything right and in order, I would be okay. But I wasn't okay. I made decisions based on expectations and what would keep me hidden and safe. I forgot about my dreams to pursue singing or living my dreams on my terms. I became cold and distant toward men. When most college girls my age were in the prime of dating and having fun exploring themselves, I didn't date much. On the rare times I did, I never allowed myself to get too attached and ensured that by only dating men who weren't completely available to me. Making it easy for me to keep parts of myself hidden. Ironically, if it didn't work, I still ended up becoming secretly possessive or obsessed over the relationship for some time afterwards.

I got real good at hiding my feelings and wearing the mask of a strong woman who pretended to not care for real affection or intimacy from men. Those were my survival muscles kicking in, protecting that six-year-old girl. Now that she was a grown woman, she could protect that little girl in a way her loved ones weren't brave enough to. The only problem was that little girl was no longer being molested, she was no longer in any real danger. She was now simply a grown woman wallowing in her own misery and creating her own suffering.

I had to make a change. As a young woman I realized I was dreadfully lonely and tired of being hidden and voiceless.

We all have survivor instincts that sustain us. God equips us with the ability to preserve ourselves, even in the midst of chaos and danger. However, you must not allow surviving past pain to keep you from experiencing present abundance. It's through self-exploration and discovering that you learn how view the lessons gained through your pain and those innate survivor skills to help you thrive.

I can't pinpoint a single situation that changed my perspective, but I always knew the survivor inside of me and that what I was going through wasn't going to consume me. I started listening to her, the survivor. Those voices in my head would tell me I could allow love in, and I could speak up for me. I started listening to those nudges, and writing down what I heard.

My grandmother, aunt, and mom raised me in the Baptist church. I remembered what the preachers taught, the songs we sang in choir and the feelings I got. I leaned on those words and through self-exploration, I started to write what I felt. The more I wrote, the more I began to feel a shift in my thoughts, my desires and my actions. I began to look at the world differently. I started to realize that I had options. I could choose the direction of my life, and could be and do anything I wanted.

I began to see my emotional challenges as opportunities to be something greater. I allowed myself to dive deeper into my pain trusting that I wouldn't break or fall apart, but instead find the desires of that six-year old little girl, and her voice. I could save her. I had to learn to talk about my pain not from a place of victim-hood but of survival and triumph. I sought help and counseling so I could develop the tools to move through it.

Know that situations happen to reveal and access something deeper in you; your purpose is trying to be birthed out of you and often uses your pain to reveal itself. We often think or allow bad things to force us to cover for safety and stay hidden in the *I'll never be this* or *I'm not meant to really be more than that*, not realizing there's a hidden blessing in our challenges.

I began to discover my voice by learning to ask for help. I

started journaling and writing more. I had always written poems, which helped me tap into my voice, but journaling allowed me to write my frustrations in present time. I revisited my love for music, wrote more songs and sang—though only to myself. At about the age of 33, God brought into my path what I call a "voice coach"—someone I trusted, who valued me, that would allow me to pour into them and would be able to pour into me. Once I discovered my voice, I began learning how to trust my voice, what I had to say, and how I say it, without apology. Through that, I discovered my purpose: to help other women discover their purpose through identification of who they uniquely are and giving them the tools to BE just that.

Today, I get to speak around the country and internationally to women about what it means to be free in spirit and in life. I write books about it, lead workshops and commit my life to educating and advocating on behalf of women who are silenced. It's my life's work. By discovering my own voice, I'm able to empower other women to do the same.

How you can learn to awaken your voice?

1. Find quiet space. No matter how hectic your life, find time to sit in quiet. Stillness—the absence of movement—brings much peace, calm and access to your voice.

2. Feed your soul. First, realize you have a soul, an essence in you that can never be hurt or violated, no matter what's done to you. It remains intact, untouched and unmolested. It's in you now, even as you read these words or recant a painful memory. That essence in you—soul and spirit—is still there, nudging at you and wanting to talk to you. Feed this with information about you. Whenever possible, talk to someone whom you trust with your story and seek knowledge about yourself through prayer, music and meditation.

3. Access your silent place through journaling. There's something about placing pen to paper that seemingly allows God to speak directly to you. Your soul begins to pour itself out on paper, revealing that soul message that was once hidden to you.

Know this: *You do not, should not, and cannot suffer in silence.* Nothing that's happened to you was meant to silence your voice. You are meant to be heard. If your current situation is silencing you, gather the tools needed so you can begin empowering yourself. Realize God is working FOR YOU and on your behalf to organize an army to awaken your voice from the depths of silence. You are not weak, and it's not normal for you to be quiet. It's beneath what God has for you. You who are made in His image, a woman who's been charged with birthing new nations. Begin to equip yourself with the three tools above. Find peace in stillness. In the midst of chaos, find quiet space so you can access the place God has given you that cannot be tampered by man. Feed that place with new knowledge (like this book) and with people you can trust who can feed you positively, and access your knowledge of Self. And write what you feel. Let your voice be heard first on paper; make that connection to that deeper aspect inside of you. Build and develop your courage muscle.

Did you know? Your vocal cords' muscles, once removed or damaged, can be rebuilt, but the unique sound of your voice cannot. The sound of voice is so unique that it is difficult to replace. It's valuable, your worth is unmatched.

You deserve to live, soar, thrive, and not die a slow death of silence.

Katrina

About Katrina

Katrina M. Harrell is a 4x best-selling author, speaker and business strategist. She is the founder of *Your Simple Bookkeeper*™ and *Business Liberation*™, *LLC.* As a business strategist, Katrina serves and supports entrepreneurs in pricing, packaging and positioning their services for optimal profit impact. A transformational speaker, an award-winning entrepreneur, and a former corporate accountant, Katrina's innovative approach to business and spiritual development has been highlighted in National Bestseller Reinventing Professional Services in the Digital Marketplace *(Ari Kaplan – JWiley),* and *Black Enterprise Magazine.* She has been named *Top 50 Black Business Women Online* by Black Business Women Online (2011 and 2012) and is the recipient of the 2013 *"Business on the Rise"* Award by Stiletto Women In Business Media.

To learn more, visit
www.KatrinaMHarrell.com

3

RHONDA "THE INNERgizer" WHITE

The Making of a Relentless Woman
– a RICH Queen!

There I was, so filled with joy, love and excitement, becoming a wife to the man I loved. ALL my life, I witnessed the epitome of a loving and graceful woman, my sweet mother, the late Ionie Grace White, being treated like a queen by my awesome dad, the late Bishop Jesse White, and I truly wanted to experience that type of love from a man.

I remember walking down the aisle with the most breathtaking custom-made dress you have ever seen in your life. As soon as the doors opened and my dad and I walked in, the audience of nearly one thousand guests gave loud "Oohs" and "Ahhs," while numerous cameras flashed, trying to capture this striking gown—which was like none other. As I began to walk with my incredible dad, I had the cordless mic under my veil, singing to my man: *"In this quiet place with you, I look into your eyes to share the deepest parts of you and you alone. I keep no secrets, for there is no thought you have not known. I give my best, and all the rest to you I lay it down. With all my heart, I want to love you and live my life each day to know you more. All that is within me is yours completely. I love you only with all my heart."*

Oh, what a glorious day for me. Twenty-seven years old, a virgin, marrying the man I had known for over six years and was engaged to for two years. I thought I knew him— no secrets—but to my surprise, after being married for a while, I discovered he was still legally married to another woman. He told me he'd never been married! I cannot explain to you the hurt, embarrassment and betrayal I felt from this man who I cherished when I discovered this shocking situation. No, he wasn't perfect, but I loved that man.

When an attorney confirmed that our marriage was null and void, as if we were never married to begin with, I broke down and cried. He begged me not to leave, to forgive him. He'd never divorced his first wife. I guess he thought it would evaporate or go away and I would never find out about it, but that was not the case. I was looking through some items for him and found a paper with her last name, which was the same as my husband's. I knew then I had to confront him when he came home. The rest is history. He couldn't believe he had left those papers in our house and that I had found them.

After I moved back to Indiana, I was very much embarrassed to face my dad's church members and those in my hometown, but I had to move on. After almost a year, he begged me to remarry him after showing me the official divorce papers from the first wife. I decided to give him another chance—only to be devastated once again, many times. When I thought my husband was traveling for his job, I later found out he had been seeing another woman for several months—after I'd agreed to remarry him! What a slap in the face! This woman also became pregnant by him while we were remarried. Following this very disappointing time in my life, I took a long break from seeing anyone. I just shut down and closed myself off to dating for a while. I had to rebuild my trust in men again because my ex-husband really did a number on me.

After a while, I met a minister at a conference out of town. We started talking on the phone and visiting each other. Sometime later, he proposed to me. We got married and moved to Atlanta where his job relocated him. About six months into the marriage, I noticed he had an anger problem that he had hidden very well. I tried to do everything he asked of me and was a great wife, but hardly anything I did pleased him. I asked one of his sisters why he was so angry and she said he never forgave their deceased mother for the things she did to them. I told her, "I am not his mother. I am trying to love him." She confessed that she had wondered how long it would take me to see the hurt in him and how he really was. She also told me he mistreated every woman who connected with him, trying to get back at their mother. Later, I found out I was his fifth wife. He is now married a sixth time!

His anger would burst forth out of nowhere. He was often very nasty, and after he tried to hit me, I asked him if we could go to counseling. He continued to refuse. I told him, "One day, you're going to come home from work and I will be gone." He didn't take me seriously, but it happened. I left and we did divorced. There I was, not even forty years old and twice-divorced. How did this happen to me? I finally had to dig deep within myself and evaluate why I was attracting these types of men in my life—men who didn't love themselves and were not capable of truly loving anyone else. I discovered that I didn't love myself as much

I thought I did. When I began to spend more time with God in prostrate prayer, asking Him to restore my hope in Him, to fill up my holes and make me whole, that's when I began to forgive and release so I could walk in peace. Only then did I begin to increase, cleanse and move forward.

During this time, I also divinely met my beautiful spiritual mother of over 12 years. I also had a mentor, who I met through the first MLM company I joined to lose the stress weight I had gained because of all I'd been through. The situations caused me to go from a size 10/12 to an 18/20 in seven months due to stress eating. I lost weight in three and a half months through cleansing and herbs my mentor told me about. She also introduced me to *The Dynamic Laws of Prosperity,* a life-changing book by Catherine Ponder, which helped me heal, mature, and go from feeling like a victim to a victor. I was also resurrected by reading *The Greatest Miracle in the World* by one of my favorite authors, Og Mandino. These books became my empowerment friends.

During all of this, my mother passed. God knew just who and what I needed when I needed it. He assured me I was not alone (Isaiah 41:9-10; Joshua 1:5-9 NLT). Thank God, He allowed me to meet my spiritual mother and mentor to be there for me here on earth.

Ladies, you cannot always stay isolated. Pray for divine protection, divine direction and divine connections, consisting of new friends and acquaintances for a new start. This will help you overcome after you have been cleansed, healed, fulfilled, and developed. Also, get to know you and love you first and foremost. Only then can you get to know and love someone else. This is one of the most important lessons I've learned. I knew I wanted a wonderful marriage. I knew that I deserved it because I was willing to give what I desired to receive.

After I finally became whole within, I felt like a brand NEW woman, ready to share my story and empower others to *"Stop crying and start flying, stop complaining and start aiming, stop talking and start walking. Make a difference, for this is the* best *day of your life!"*

I began to turn my tragedies into true triumphs when God birthed massive amounts of creativity through me in the form of, to name a few, The Eagle Women's Monthly Network; the Annual Interdenominational Women's Revival and Fellowship; a weekly TV show, Soaring Eagles with Rhonda White hosted on TCT; a 12-city Relation-SHIP Tour; a columnist for various newspapers and magazines; publisher of four books and three CDs, all released on the same day; Elevation Speaker/Coach; an herbalist, conducting Rest and Silence Retreats; and the birth of over 14 online networking sites, including MarketingUDaily.com and SacredSoaringSingles.com.

RICH Queen, I want you to know that *your treasures are hidden in the tragedies of your life!* Had I never experienced what I went through, I wouldn't have much to say to help create a forest-fire desire in others to soar higher, no matter what they've gone through. Remember, our "to" will always be much better than what we "go through."

RICH Queen, this was the beginning of my new beginning. In spite of all the things I had been through, I still had joy. Truly, this journey has been one of stretching and development, like a rubber band and the making of a Relentless Woman.

What does the word Relentless mean?

It means to be:

- Determined and definite in your direction.

- Persistent and consistent.

- Continual and perpetual.

- Remaining and enduring.

- Loyal, lasting and loving.

- Dependable and devoted.

- Trustworthy and permanent.

- Faithful and stable.

- Uncompromising and unwavering.

- Unshakable... RICH Queen, that's God and that's YOU!

The only way I made it through these shocking events, including the planning of a suicide in the '90s, is by the Grace of my Almighty God. When you uncover, discover and launch your *Giant of Potential* within and begin to impact and help others, your life will shift and your MONIES will spring forth because you are not afraid to share your TestiMONIES.

As women, we are like rubber bands: We are durable and can endure some of the most difficult situations with flexibility and versatility. RICH Queen, remember that just like a rubber band, God cannot use you until you have been stretched. We were all made to hold together things that are bigger than ourselves, just like a rubber band. And like a rubber band, when it sits in a drawer, not being used for a while, it'll dry out and become hard; when stretched, it'll snap easily. Ladies, just know we are made with good stuff. That's why we have been through *so much*. We can handle becoming better, not bitter. Everything in life must go through a process to be used. Grapes for wine and juice; cotton for clothes; trees to build houses; olives for oil; and peanuts to make cardboard, dye, penicillin, and peanut butter. So take your process with a smile, for your process has been preparing you for your purpose. Be at peace. Don't fight your process, write your process and enjoy your journey—for you've made it!

Finally, RICH Queen, here are three things I encourage you to do to help you not only soar through the storm, but also take the world by storm:

1. **Truly become aware of who you are, whose you are and what valuables are inside of you.** You are a RICH Queen, more valuable than Tiffany's!

Becoming aware of these truths will cause you to be a force to be reckoned with and make you a positive magnet to start attracting what and who you really desire in your life. One of my favorite authors, James Allen, has a great quote: *"Men and women do not attract what they want, but they attract that which they are!"* It's a hard pill to swallow, but needed. Another one of my favorite authors, Og Mandino, wrote a book, *The Greatest Miracle in the World*; that is a must-read for you. I also encourage you to get a coach to help you through your past and help you maximize your present and future.

Also, keep in mind one of the quotes God gave me:

"Don't you dare let your past paralyze your potential. Honor it and learn from it, but then let it go so that you can grow!"

2. **"Invest in Y.O.U. Inc.,** the BEST company you will ever INvest in!"

Y: **Yearning** · You must have a yearning or passion in life and walk in it every day.

O: **Open** · You must be open and teachable to release what and who you don't need from your life. Be open to receive what and who you *do* need!

U: **Unique** · You have a unique fingerprint that no one in the world has. Out of the millions born before you, out of over seven billion people on the planet, out of all the millions who will be born after you die, no one can EVER duplicate your fingerprint! There is something assigned to your fingerprint that only you can do like YOU. No copies exists; you are it. So, why not be the best YOU that you can be?

Remember this:
"The day you were born, you were PUSHED into the atmosphere to release your greatness to the world; I am so glad you showed up! So you cannot give up!" Someone needs what God breathed inside of you to do.

3. **Build and develop your vertical relation-SHIP with God, second to NONE!** I don't care what you do or what others say, never, ever try to replace the Almighty God with anyone or anything. You will regret it. I've discovered that learning more about and spending time alone with God is the best Relation-

SHIP you will ever have. He will never let you down. He always knows and wants the best for you, and He will never lie to or hurt you.

You are His special treasure and most precious possession. ⁻ (Deuteronomy 7:6; Zechariah 2:8).

I'm so excited about your future. What about you? I expect to see great things from you and look forward to helping catapult you to reach heights unknown in your life. Now, SOAR2More!

About Rhonda

Rhonda White, CNHP is a mega-entrepreneur, author, radio host, speaker, and coach. As a certified natural health professional, she specializes in herbal medicine and has helped many people to be proactive rather than reactive with their health and wholeness. She is widely-known as **"The INNERgizer"** and loves to catapult others to uncover, discover and launch their *Giant of Potential* within. She is one of the most sought-after speakers, traveling over 20 years as a Change Agent to numerous colleges, schools, companies, conventions and churches (including Bishop T.D. Jakes' The Potter's House). Additionally, she has hosted her own TV and radio shows, including *TCT Live,* reaching over 100 million worldwide.

To learn more, visit
www.RhondaWhite.com

4

KEYNA McCLINEK

911: Rescued From Hurt to Happiness

The memory of that day will forever be imprinted on my heart. When it first happened, I thought I'd relive it each day. The agony. The emotional damage. Has your world ever flipped upside down? I felt as if I'd never sleep again, as if my eyes would be mired open forever. It took all of thirty minutes for the heart-sized bubble my family and I lived in to be popped. It took just that little amount of time for all of our hearts to be shaken and shattered. None of us would ever be emotionally complete again, and some of our bodies would never be restored to their former positions and conditions.

On March 9, 2009, the cool steel awakened my soul. Usually, I can wake myself up, but this time, my eyes wouldn't open. Not until the pistol was shoved further in my cheek, and I heard one of the deepest male tones telling me to wake up. Again, my eyes refused to open. I lay there, my body as stiff as a board. This must've angered him because he shook me. "Wake up," vibrated through my ears. Immediately, I wanted to call for my mother, but all I could get out was, *"Mmooooo---"* before he snatched my arm and told me to shut up. I was terrified; not because he had the gun to my face, but because I thought he wanted to rape me. All I ever wore to bed was a T-shirt and underwear, so he could've done so easily. I pushed him away and started saying things I can't remember. It was like I no longer noticed the gun that sat softly against my cheek.

But those weren't his intentions at all. He knew what he'd come for and what he would get. Well, *attempt* to get. It was then that I noticed a second person standing in the blackout that was my room. The man with the pistol left me with his partner in crime. I didn't dare say anything because I didn't want to startle my younger sister and stepbrother. After all, waking up to that sent my heart from its rightful position down into my toes. I knew that for two younger children, this would be something that stuck with them for life. Not that it isn't stuck to my soul like glue, but better me than all three of us. I positioned my face into the beginning of the sunrise as morning was soon coming. My dirty looks cut his conscience like the thin ray of light cut the darkness in the room. He chose to scuttle out as if he had second thoughts and jumped over the banister, only to stumble down the steps. Still, he made a successful exit.

I searched for my phone, which was about to go off soon to wake me up for school. It was always under my pillow, but the alertness that the gun forced upon me caused it to fall under my bed. When I got it, I couldn't dial 911 fast enough. Then, there was the first shot. Second. Third. Fourth. I lost count. In the midst of me answering the millions of questions the operator had, there were a billion things going on in my head. My mom was busy projecting obscenities as if there weren't bullets piercing her skin. I wanted to help and cry out for her. I'm assuming I answered enough questions because as I recall, I just ran for her. The foolish hooligan locked himself in the bedroom and, as his pistol emptied, he worried about what may have happened next. His only way out was to break the door, and he did. A few big bangs got him his freedom and a chance for me to see my mother for what I thought would be my last time.

She called for me to back away. Even as the criminal gave me the look of death, I knew he could do nothing. I wouldn't allow him and his shenanigans to take over my household. Ignoring my mother, I attempted to get into her room, but the way he broke out of the door prohibited me from doing so. All I saw was blood, but I couldn't tell from where or whether it was from my mother or her lover. The door was still on its hinges. The escape hole he made was enough for him to break free but would have cut my whole body if I even tried to go in. Instead, I talked to them. Although her lover wasn't my biological father, he was the best father figure. I had them repeat their names, something funny, and the three words I would've wanted burned into my brain if this was our last conversation, "I love you."

The ambulances and police officers rushed in after what felt like an eternity, but was really only a few minutes. Between checking on the victims, I made sure my sister and stepbrother remained calm and sleeping. With the business of help running rapidly through our small apartment, my sister woke up. All I could do was hold and protect her from seeing my mother in her condition. Honestly, I don't think I wanted to see her like that either. As they carried her down the steps, she said it one last time, "I love you." I grabbed my sister tighter and tried to reassure her as I saw worry and confusion all over her face. As they dragged my stepfather out next, I let go of my sister and had a conversation with the police, one that angered me. Instead of being worried about the invasion and the criminals, they were more worried about the victims and what they saw around the house.

At this point, my heart was aching and my head was throbbing. I decided to ignore them and woke my brother up. I took snacks and juice to my aunt's apartment downstairs for my siblings. I agreed to go to the precinct, hoping they'd help my mother and stepfather. Nothing much changed. As the story made the 6 A.M. news report, the calls started pouring in. I answered for a few family members as well as the family of my stepfather, telling them a rushed version of what happened. Immediate family had arrived to the hospital before me, and I was relieved to see them. There was a great deal of drama that concluded with the isolation of us from my family, so I assumed no one would be there. At the sight of my cousin, I took a deep breath, asked about my mother and was told she was okay. I took a minute to myself, allowing the tears to rush down my face like ocean waves crashing into the rocks in the sand.

It was like there was a slide show of the experience in my brain and no matter what else I thought about, it remained at the forefront. As more people found out my mother and stepfather had been shot, the halls flooded. Some with genuine concern and care, others wanting to see them at their worst to report back to the streets any news they could soak up. I had her list shut down. There were six people who could come in and out, everyone else needed my permission. In the midst of this visitor lockdown, my body shut down. I could no longer ignore the soreness of my soul. Every part of my body ached and as soon as my cousin took my sister away for a bit, I let go of myself completely. I asked myself a thousand questions similar to those the operator had asked me on the phone; questions I had no real answers for because the doctors told me she was okay. I forced myself to believe the worst of things.

I'll never forget seeing my mother like that. The bottom of her beautiful, brown face ripped apart by a bullet, leaving a chunk of her chin hanging by one last piece of skin. Her arm dangled beside the bed as one of her main veins was split. Her chest and back punctured, prohibiting her from breathing or moving on her own. Her hair lay lifeless on her head, little strands across her face. That's how she laid right in front of me, but all I remembered was her beauty. The doctor told me he had never had such a strong patient; she was able to wait patiently for surgery with little agitation. He also said something that will stick with me forever, "Sometimes, I am never one-hundred percent with the information I give the families; however, your mother is going to be okay. She is a very strong woman, she keeps saying she has to live for her children. With her strength and the surgeries, she will be alright. I can promise you that."

Still, I cried, letting it all out. My brother was arriving from placement the next day and although he was tough, seeing his queen in that state would make him crumble. That's exactly what he did. I've never seen him so broken; his bottom lip trembled uncontrollably and before he even fell, I had my hands out to catch him to hold him, to console him. I knew I had to be the big sister who kept it together, so crying in solitude kept me sane in front of everyone. I wanted to burst into tears like we did when we were younger if one of us was being punished. Instead, I told him everything would be okay and that mom was okay. Truthfully, I had no idea what the outcome of this situation would be. I held his hand and guided him back to my mother's room where we tried to create a normal scene, as if we were all in her bedroom, laughing and joking. Only this time, we fed her ice chips and tried really hard not to stare at her wounds.

I didn't want my mom to talk, so I talked to her. When I touched her hand, I felt the strength that she and doctors spoke of. It was like something electrified my soul. I knew my mother was trying to fight for her life after having eight bullets penetrate her chest, face, back, and arm; so I needed to be strong, too. Not for other people to lay on my shoulder crying, but for once, I needed to be strong for me. I couldn't stop the tears from flowing, no matter what I thought about or where I was. All I wanted was for my mother to look and feel better. In order for her to get better, I continued living almost as if this never happened.

I had the greatest support system at school. My friends knew something was wrong the day it happened because I was nowhere to be found. After calling my phone all morning, they left school and rushed to the hospital. They saw my mother as if she was their own and stayed by our sides. At first, letting out their own sorrow, then shifting gears to make me laugh about all the funny and crazy things my mom ever said to us. They're a huge reason why I was comfortable when I went back to school. Everyone else stared at me as if they'd seen a ghost, like it was too early for me to be walking the hallways. In the back of my mind, I felt the same way, but the SATs were right around the corner and grades were being sent in for the quarter soon.

My principal called me into his office to share a similar event he'd undergone. He was very empathetic and able to sympathize with me because he too had a pistol shined in his face. He agreed to freeze my grades if I needed to take time off, but I declined. Time away from school would just push me into a depressed and nervous state of mind. Of course, I looked over my shoulder, walking to and from the subway or bus stations, and I was a jittery mess whenever I heard loud sounds, but school was like a second family to me. Being around them helped me believe I'd get through this. My school was so amazing and loving that they even suggested raising money for me, but I declined. We were a family who'd experienced a shocking situation, not a family in need of money.

My teachers didn't know how to react to my presence in the classroom, but I knew I had something to prove. I pledged to myself that I wouldn't let the urban neighborhoods that surrounded me define who I wanted to be in life. I knew I had greater callings. I had so much I wanted to achieve that, one way or another, I'd make my mother proud. Finishing strong was so important to me. It was generous that people cared for and helped me in a time of need, but the only real way I'd rise above my experience was to help myself.

I forced myself to see the good that came out of this situation. My family was there for my mother every step of the way. It taught me who my real friends were and that no matter where life took us, I could always count on them.

The biggest lesson was my *ability to turn my hurt into happiness.* When I was happy, my mother absorbed my positive energy. When my mom was released from the hospital, she was having issues with her self-image due to her scars. I was happy enough for me, but I was also happy and confident enough to help her get her confidence back.

"You're a true beauty," is what she always reminded me, and I reminded her of the same.

I snatched my life back, continued going out with my friends and enjoying myself. *My pain was the driving force of my progression.* I grew up being told I would be better. My mother gave me a life she wasn't afforded. For that, I'll always appreciate and love her. I ultimately found my love for the union of the pad and pen, and my knack for learning. I promised myself I would never let either go.

Experiencing this home invasion could have erupted my plans to attend the number one HBCU in the country, but I didn't allow it to. As I walk across that stage May 18, 2014, I'll remember the hurt and pain from that day, but will feel happiness and be proud of my progression—as *my shocking situation is a part of me, but will never define me.*

About Keyna

Keyna McClinek is a graduating senior at Spelman College, majoring in Psychology. Having faced many adversities, she began to view education as her only outlet to refrain from a world of ignorance. She aspires to be a Child Psychologist in addition to fulfilling her multi-passions in teaching, motivational speaking and charity work. She is highly ambitious and determined not to allow future hardships to prevent her from achieving her dreams.

To learn more, visit
www.About.me/KeynaMcClinek

5

DR. JANICE ARMSTRONG

Screaming At My Stress

A s I sat on the side of my bed, all of the noise seemed muffled and I felt as if I was going to pass out. My body got warm and I felt a bit dizzy. It was, I imagine, similar to an out-of-body experience. I sat there, numb, mentally distancing myself from all of the confusion around me. Everything seemed to be at a standstill, very quiet and then a loud, wailing sound brought me back to reality. Oddly enough, I was the one wailing loudly. I was so overwhelmed that I needed one good scream to make the confusion go away, if just for a moment.

My son, who was just over two years old, started crying because I scared the mess out of him and my infant daughter continued to cry uncomfortably from who knows what. I was still trying to figure out her three-month-old mannerisms. I thought to myself, *"Could it be THIS hard? I have done this before."* What should have been a piece of cake, surely wasn't, and it was in that moment of temporary breakdown that I realized I was in over my head and I had no choice but to change. Now don't get me wrong, I love my children. I love *the love* that created them and I love my husband who has helped me raise them, but I would be lying if I said that the early months with my two toddlers were an easy feat.

The day after my "survival scream," I realized it was my saving grace. Even though I unintentionally scared my babies, *I shouted down the pain* and inadequacy I was feeling at that time—and it felt good. I just wanted to sit and stay there, silent, but my circumstances didn't allow that to be possible. This was more than the baby blues; it was three months after birth. See, I had the baby blues with my son and I knew this situation was different. I knew "this" wasn't me. I realized that my stressors contributed to the postpartum depression and I needed to get a grip! This was not the first time I'd felt that way. The dizziness and the feelings of being overwhelmed knocked me to the floor before, but this time, I recognized what it was. I knew that stress was the monkey on my back when it happened with my children. I refused to let it overtake me because I had a lot more at stake: caring for my babies. They needed me, my husband needed me, but I just couldn't muster the energy I used to have.

When I was a young, vibrant, college student, I remember being in my dorm room, talking to a friend about final exams. I was overwhelmed. My first semester was wonderful! It felt like a review of my senior year in high school, but the second semester was not like that at all. I tried to venture out and have fun without a decent plan of action to balance it well with my studies. I thought I had it together, but found out quickly that I was falling apart. It was the end of the semester and I couldn't clean up the mess I'd made. I needed to study hard and long, so an all-nighter was necessary. My friend introduced me to Jolt Cola, a drink equivalent to three to four cups of coffee. I was wired and I stayed up for over 24 hours straight—craziness, indeed! I was up all night and all day as I took my tests and began to study for my next exams. I came into my room from the library and my friend was still awake in her room. I knocked on the door and sat on her bed. She told me I looked a mess, which I'm sure I did. Suddenly, I started to feel dizzy and completely blacked out.

I woke up hours later, in the early afternoon, in her bed. "It's about time you got up," she said. I looked at my watch and realized I was three hours away from my next exam and I had yet to study. I started to hyperventilate and my heart raced. I ran to my room and gathered my next set of books, trying to do something...anything! What that was going to be? Who knows, but something had to be done! I tried to study and about an hour in, I screamed, throwing my books and papers around hysterically. My friend rushed into my room and tried to calm me down. Next thing I knew, a gush of water slapped me in my face. I 'woke' up. At that moment, I was not myself. I had no control. I fell to my knees and began to cry while my friend hugged me and told me it would be alright. I eventually stood up and got into the shower. I remember the warmth of the water, the feeling of my woes leaving me and washing down the drain. I realized how cleansing the water was, the funk of an entire day that I chose to dedicate to my books and not to my body washing away.

I got dressed and walked to my class. For the next two hours, I faced the challenge of my test...and failed. Oh well. I created this mess and had no one to blame but myself. I learned my lesson that day and I made the necessary changes to make it right, but that wasn't the end of my anxiety journey. In the midst of my many activities as an undergraduate student, I had to continue learning how to adjust. I had to determine when I needed help and how to ask for it. However, my pride kept me from doing so. I would ultimately realize that this was how I functioned, and it wasn't a positive habit.

Once I set my pride aside, I sought help with a professional.

The first suggestion given was to take medication. "What?! You have GOT to be kidding me! That can't be the only solution," I thought. I was a psychology major and well aware that behavior modification was an option. More specifically, relaxation exercises would work. It HAD to work. I made it work. I sought out what I loved to do and the music I loved to listen to. For me, it was none other than hip-hop dance and hip-hop music. I would retreat to my room and blast my joints while in the hot shower, washing away the mess that stressed me. I listened to groups like Wu-Tang Clan, NWA and Onyx—hardcore groups that helped me *let off steam while relaxing in steam*. I'd rap at the top of my lungs, gritting my teeth, flinging water everywhere. Some would say I was crazy, but it was my outlet.

I screamed, screamed, SCREAMED at the top of my lungs as I realized the strongholds that bound me. In 1995, I didn't understand how important releasing was, but the incident in 2012 was yet another opportunity to put it into practice. In the midst of all I had faced during that time: getting married, going back to school for graduate and doctoral studies, having two babies, buying homes, changing jobs, etc. (all good, but potential stressors), I found Jesus Christ again. That was the difference I found in those seventeen years. I have always loved the Lord, but certain circumstances made me stray from His guidance. My husband, Jay redirected me, helping me to realize that I shouldn't fall to my knees because I was totally overwhelmed and had to resort to throwing papers and a book, but that I should fall because I needed to submit to the *One* who can take care of it all. I had to shout unto *The* Lord and invite Him to save me—figuratively, literally and spiritually.

So on the side of my bed, my scream was a cry for help. It

was my attempt to let go of my feelings of inadequacy, a way to cleanse my mind of the erroneous thoughts of doubt, dread, and the question of "Why me?" It was an opportunity to start over. It was revealing; it was honest. It made me realize that I WAS CRAZY! I was crazy to think that God would give me more than I could handle. I was crazy to think that I could not be a wonderful mother to my children. I was crazy to think that I couldn't be a wonderful wife. I was crazy to think that I didn't have the strength to do it all. I have done it, I did do it, and I continue to do it. I thought my "survival scream" was my saving grace, but no. It was really a reminder of who my saving grace really was: God.

As I think back on those times of anxiety, I realize that when my husband took me to the beach or to the docks, I would just sit in the sun by the water. I would listen to the waves or watch the seagulls fly over me. It was peaceful. I remember once, while in my doctoral program, I was out on the deck of our oceanfront hotel room when Jay came up behind me and said, "You're watching God!" It all made sense.

Though I didn't understand why the warm water made me feel better that day in my dorm room shower, I surely understand it now. Water renews us. To overcome my anxiety, feelings of inadequacy and my depression, I went to the living word, I went to the water. I used it to wash away my woes and I was content in Christ.

In order to overcome my anxiety challenge, I realized:

- I could change.
- I had to want to change.
- I had to be honest with myself.

- I needed to trust the help and assistance of others.
- I have control of my decisions.
- I needed to accept the consequences of those decisions.
- If the solutions to my problems are beyond my scope, God waits for me to turn it over to Him.
- Screaming at my stress makes me depend on the Lord more than on myself.

Do I still experience anxiety? Of course I do, but I realize it's only temporary and that God has filled me with what I need to overcome. He created a purpose for my life to educate others on the consequences of living a stress-filled life. I get to address different audiences, from youth to counseling professionals, about my life-changing experience and offer solutions. Never did I think that such craziness in my life would grow into a benefit for me and for the lives of others. Yes, I still bump some classic "old skool" hip hop from time to time because it gets me pumped, hyped, and I dance my pain away. But now, I have a more powerful addition to my stress management: knowing God and screaming at the top of my lungs, declaring that the spirit of anxiety will *not* win against the spirit of Christ!

I tell you this: *Scream at your stress!* Tell it who's boss! If you can't handle it, there is a bigger boss who can. That spirit of anxiety knows who He is and surely doesn't want to mess with Him. Dismiss your stressful lifestyle and revisit what you enjoy and who you are.

Let the *living water* rid you of your stress. Let it renew you, cleanse you. The two parts hydrogen and one part oxygen contains one part the Father, one part the Son, and one part the Holy Spirit. Dasani®, Aquafina® or VOSS has anything on the Boss! If you can't dismiss stress, let Him fire it for you. I promise you, the cleansing will be worth it because you are.

Express from your chest and scream away your stress!

Dr. Jai

About Dr. Jai

So much to say about Dr. Jai in so little space and time, so let's do it with a little rhyme! Janice "Dr. Jai" Armstrong is a leadership consultant, motivational speaker and coach. Holding a doctoral degree in Strategic Leadership, she offers a wealth of personal and professional development information to her audience. She's also the author of *"From the Street to the Executive Suite: Remixing Street Smarts and Life Lessons into Leadership Success!"* and the creator of Sexy Leadership™, making leadership concepts more attractive.

To learn more, visit
www.LiHKLeaders.com

6

TARINNA TERRELL

Triumphing Over Pain Addiction

Sometimes, you can't see the pain, but you surely can feel it. I've had my share of windy experiences that jilted and tilted me; my whole being shook. I endured many windy situations and I'm still standing strong. My memories are traumatic and I had nightmares, even up until adulthood. I could still hear the screams of a loved one being raped as I helplessly stood by the door. Whew...the peril! I kept that entire trauma in. I kept my innermost emotions inside and lived in fear. I really began to withdraw.

Many have their own stories, but this is mine. In my head, I kept the visions of a loved one high on a hallucinogen or saw them use drugs. One traumatic event after another played in my mind, but I remained silent. I kept all of my fears to myself, and in return, I didn't learn how to trust. The foundation of secrets and non-trust seeped into my heart from an early age and I could not love or trust those close to me. Therefore, I surely couldn't trust a stranger. I always created an arm's length distance between myself and others.

For years, I was quiet as a lamb, suffering in silence. May I suggest that silence is not golden? I was often in isolation, withdrawn and aloof. I was a walking corpse. I talked about nothing; however, my nightmares were very vocal. I suppressed so many memories that it caused emotional damage, which prevented me from really sharing and getting close to anyone. I was a good, wholesome, clean church girl with dark secrets and a picturesque imagination. I remained silent, refusing to talk about it.

I refused to share how the inappropriate touches affected me. I refused to share how the sexual assault I heard affected my psyche. I refused to share how I was afraid to be alone. I refused to share how I didn't trust men. I refused to share that I often wondered why men didn't want to violate me; I kind of expected it. My mind was a cesspool, and some part of me thought this was supposed to happen. I refused to share how I wrestled with my sexual identity because all the events that happened to me as a young, innocent child confused me. I became an adult in a child's body. On the outside looking in, I excelled and was the "different" one. All was a farce. I should have won an Oscar for Best Actress in a Dramatic Series, talk about a real life *Scandal*. The award would've been very auspicious as I was a master at pretending. I did not talk about it.

I ended up getting pregnant before I got married. I couldn't live with that, so I opted to cover up the shame. I remember saying, "Getting married can't be any worse than being pregnant and not married." As a result, I tied the knot while I was four months pregnant and even wore a girdle so my baby bump wouldn't show. There were many unwed women in my family, and I felt pressure to be different. However, I wasn't different. My thought processes were tragic. For years, I lived in shame after entering into a covenant I didn't want to be in.

While married, I endured domestic violence, both verbal and emotional. I suffered through infidelity, mistrust and so much more. These painful situations resulted in me dealing with the police, lawyers, the court system, and therapists. I cycled into an abyss of toxicity and I stayed in it for a long period of time because it became my addiction. Honestly, I really liked the attention; many of my wounds were self-inflicted. I had attracted the very thing that was in me.

I remained unhappily married for several years, but it wasn't all my ex-husband's fault. The drama in my marriage began because I had no understanding of who I was. Had I known, I wouldn't have gotten married. I was literally trying to fit a square peg into a circle, but no matter how I tried, it just wasn't going to fit. I did what religion says: pray and the person will change. I prayed that my former husband would change, but the relationship dissolved. Although I was unhappy, I had become addicted to the pain because it was all so familiar to me. Since my painful situations started at an early age, that's what I knew. So I stayed where I was comfortable. Day after day, I continued to inject myself with more and more pain because my innermost being was in pain. I kept feeding it like it was a baby and it kept growing and intensifying. Today, I am more aware and enlightened, and I realize that I was the one who needed to change. I needed to be truthful with me and walk in my own integrity. And once I got an understanding of who I was created to be, the shift happened in my life.

Triumphing after tragedy requires that you *Talk* about it, be *Resilient,* walk in *Integrity,* develop an *Understanding,* be *Motivated,* find your *Purpose,* and be *Hopeful*. These are the ingredients to being triumphant. Yes, tragedies will happen, but following these key principles will help you:

"T"

Talk. Talking was the one thing I needed. The healing began when I started talking about my past issues and experiences. I had to let out all the toxins of the past in order to allow new, life-giving information in. I found safe places to share and I encourage you to do the same. Talking about it saved my life.

"R"

Resilient. Anyone who endures any type of hardship has resiliency at the core of their being. Unfortunately, many do not survive tragedies. Those who have experienced traumatic circumstances such as rape, abuse, molestation, or domestic violence are sometimes mentally and emotionally dead. Many don't make it and literally, physically die.

My blood line is rich with resilient woman, particularly my mother and a favorite aunt. They raised me to be resilient and strong and taught me to keep pushing and to never give up like the many women throughout the world who exhume strength and courage to continue living. There were many days I didn't feel strong. Often, in the midst of a storm, you can't see your strength. However, when the storm passes, you see what you're made of. I often ask, "Why didn't I turn to drugs? Why didn't I become sexually promiscuous? Why didn't I commit suicide?" I must say my faith sustained me. It truly wasn't any of my own doing. In addition, I had a great support system; strong women surrounded me.

I believe that your circle of influence can play a positive role in your life. *Being around strong people inadvertently gives you strength.* I was around survivors. Each word of encouragement and strength my support system shared, dripped into the core of my being like an IV. I connected with strong people, and resiliency dripped into my heart daily. That gave me life.

"I"

Integrity. I couldn't walk in my triumph until I stopped pretending. By entering a marriage I didn't want or need, I was living a lie. I was a dressed up garbage can, a well-manicured and blinged-out trash can. I was spinning out of control and I was mentally unraveling. My heart was in a hostage situation. I couldn't fully walk in integrity because I was holding secrets and being someone I was not. I was afraid to be me and afraid of being judged. I finally figured out that I had to be honest with myself and walk in my own integrity. I had to make a transformation within myself.

"U"

Understanding. Many days, I had no understanding of why I had to experience certain things. I often lamented greatly because I had to go through so much pain. However, it became my biggest motivator. Dealing with painful situations gave me the most insight and clarity. It was only when my heart was broken significantly and I was at my most vulnerable and naked self, that I began to realize I was attached to pain. Once I understood who I was destined to be, a transformation occurred in my life and I was able to move forward.

"M"

Motivation! Many days, I had no motivation at all. My energy was low, I was not optimistic, and my aura was fragile and unstable.

I believe you are what you eat, both physically and spiritually. You won't walk in the motivational realm if you're not around others who are motivated. It's just impossible. At one point, my circle was filled with people just mulling along, and I was doing the same thing. Once I changed my circle and started seeking out those who were motivated, I, too, became motivated. It was quite contagious. A young lady I know helped me get motivated from afar. She had her own fitness company, was grinding daily and also was very positive. I saw her motivational Facebook posts and that gave me the courage to change. I felt I couldn't post negativity with all her positive posts hitting the news feed. So I decided that I was either going to change or I would delete her as a Facebook friend. I decided to change and with daily hard work, my motivation increased. I had to do a mental overhaul and purge myself first. The purging of negativity and toxins from my emotional being gave me the energy to start moving forward.

"P"

Purpose. In my opinion, your trials and tribulations birth your purpose. That is why many do not find it; they give up in the battle. They throw the white flag in because the pain becomes unbearable. I thought of calling it quits many days because I wanted the emotional pain to be over. Especially during my separation and divorce process, I really wanted to die. But I couldn't fathom me being gone and my kids having to live with that, so I contemplated a way we could all go. I literally had to pull over in my car because I was afraid that if I hit the accelerator, I would drive us off the bridge. At that time, I was in a tragic mental state.

Now, as you see, I'm talking about my purpose today. I clearly know it. You can find yours, too. The journey you endured happened for a specific reason. It was designed to help you find your purpose, then help others reach theirs. Purpose-driven folks aren't selfish; they're committed to uplifting and building others. They're grateful and must share their journeys to serve others. Purpose-driven people give back and are interested in the soul of humanity. Your tragedy can turn into your purpose, just as it did for me and many others.

"H"

Hope. I always wanted to do something good in this world. In the core of my being, I desired to do something that would make a difference. I had no idea how I would accomplish this, but I hoped my education would lead me there. The one thing I could count on was my intellect. I always said it would take me far. While it has been beneficial, my honesty about how I felt in my soul has taken me even further.

Having hope is so very necessary. Even if you don't see the light, a little glimmer of hope can keep you moving in many regards. Hope says, "Although it may look this way, I still want something else." What are you hoping for? Whatever it is, I encourage you to write those things down. Hope says, "I don't want to stay where I am." Even when I was in many painful cycles, deep inside, I hoped I could get out. I didn't have the tools to get myself out because doubt took over.

Doubt is the enemy of hope. They fight each other daily. Hope pushes you while doubt paralyzes you to your core. An ounce of hope can be the thing you need to get you over a hurdle. Hope may be the only thing you have on many days. Often, there's a struggle to hope when darkness is on your back. Gratefully, I have found out that hope prevails.

We all will have a plight in life. As a matter of fact, we'll have several and should view them as lesson-learners. There is a message in each storm you experience. Attempting to escape the process won't build your internal muscle. These situations help develop your emotional and spiritual core, and they occur to feed your soul. My soul is the driving force. I surely love to adorn my outer self, but I first feed my soul and spirit.

I encourage you to tap into your inner self and to dig deep. *Be real with yourself, but don't get stuck.* People may have done things to you, but you ultimately control how you respond to what has happened. *You do have a choice: You can choose to be happy or sad.* It all boils down to your decision. I finally reached a point where I was tired of the pain and tired of being a pain addict. While people put pain on me, I realized I had a choice. I accepted the wrong that was done to me by others and broke the cycle of pain and the learned behavior of hurting.

Pain is inevitable, but suffering is a choice. I started hurting myself because that's what I saw. However, because I wanted something different, I had to do something different. I had to do an overhaul. I had to change people, places and things; ultimately, this process began with me. It has helped me share my hidden story with the world.

Today, I can boldly declare that *there is triumph after tragedy.*

Tarinna

About Tarinna

Tarinna N. Terrell is the mother of two beautiful sons, a Level II Certified Addiction Counselor, trainer, author, and poet. She self-published her first book of poems entitled *It's Time for You to Soar* and has been a featured poet on Joe's Place on WHUR Howard University Radio, Listen Vision Radio, WRTR Radio, and other local radio shows in the DC/Baltimore area. Tarinna's mission is to use poetry as a means to proclaim her personal motto that **"There is triumph after tragedy."** Her personal philosophy is that of a butterfly, in which we all have cocooned experiences, and that we evolve and birth at the appointed time.

To learn more, visit
www.TarinnaTerrell.com

7

LISA FEGGANS—ODOM

I Am Who I Never Imagined I Would Be

"You can't just sit there and wait for people to give you that golden dream, you've got to get out there and make it happen yourself." - Diana Ross

Middle children often feel left out and invisible, a contrast from their older and younger siblings. Sometimes, I felt that way because I'd always considered myself the talentless one out of all my siblings. They are all so talented. On a daily basis, I would ask God, *"What is my purpose? Why am I here? What should I be doing?"* Up to that point, I thought it was going from job to job.

My defining moment in life came one day as I contemplated the areas I was unhappy with. My job seemed to be the one area that kept flashing warning signs in my head, but I persevered. Could I have gotten another one? Yes. Did I want to? No. Even though I've always been able to find one with ease, looking for jobs is a hassle. So I sat at that desk for two years and life was relatively good until I was confronted head on with workplace bullying. When I first started that job, it was all I bragged about. I loved it, didn't want to leave when it was time for my shift to end, but after the second year, it started to change. The atmosphere became more inhibited, the people in charge more controlling. I've always danced to the beat of my own drum, never followed the crowd—it just wasn't my style. So when people around me try to control my every move, it's never a good thing. Yes, change is good, but it's not always in your best interest. I didn't agree with the changes implicated, so I became a rebel for my human dignity. My supervisor didn't like it one bit. She was covetous, insecure, miserable, desperate, distrustful, and demanding. Her awful behavior poisoned the entire department's disposition. The camaraderie among fellow teammates slowly dissipated leaving discord in its wake. The more power they gave her, the worse she became. She hated me because I wasn't pushed around so easily. Any way she could sabotage me, she tried it. Outwardly, I took whatever she threw my way with a smile which seemed to bother her a lot.

When you don't give people the ammunition to feed off of your dissatisfaction, their discontent peaks to its highest and they will try anything to bring you down. Anything.

The mentality of the people in my department was unbelievably yielding. They didn't seem to mind that their every move was being dictated. They just continued to work, eager to please, afraid to voice an opinion or show any backbone. I'm just not that person. Honestly, I felt like I was being set up to fail. With the new policies and endless delegation, it was like management was looking to weed people out slowly, but surely.

Quality no longer mattered, workmanship no longer mattered, your morals no longer mattered; it was all about the numbers. As long as your numbers were high, you were rewarded. Unless of course you were me. If your numbers dropped, you weren't doing your job. With the changes in policy, also came a change of environment. They began talk of moving into a new building, becoming more of a call center. I didn't like call centers, it wasn't part of my job description and I wanted no part. Unfortunately, I didn't have a plan. Money was tight. I couldn't just leave my job and hope a new one would fall into my lap. So I continued on, miserable, irritated and unmotivated to perform as usual. I was irritated that I found myself stuck in this situation to begin with, and miserable because I was working against my own moral compass.

Initially, to manage the situation, I just did my job, kept to myself and stayed under the radar. But trouble always has a way of finding us. To control this 'issue,' she enlisted co-workers to spy on us. Actually, spy on us and report back with anything she could use to send us packing. One co-worker was bold. She sat right next to me while the supervisor called her every morning for a report on everyone. I was absolutely astonished by the audacity of this person that sat right next to me, whispering into her phone every morning to give her daily report.

Finally, the day to move came and I decided, *new building, new attitude.* I was going to keep my head up and hopes high. Eventually we settled into our new office and things appeared fine, but soon after, she was back to her old tricks of obsessing on only me. One day, she called a meeting. Apparently everyone in the department was invited except for me. I didn't understand how exactly I had become the focus of this woman's vindictive intention. I didn't do anything wrong. I didn't suck up to her, but I performed my work effectively and efficiently each day. As each one of my co-workers went into the room where the meeting was being held, all of my co-workers were staring at me, poker-faced. I sat at my desk in total disbelief, as I couldn't believe that one person could have this much negative influence on others. I wondered, "How could one measly person turn an entire team of people against you for no apparent reason?" Shock doesn't even begin to describe how I felt. I was hurt, angry and beset by confusion.

I felt like I was in high school all over again, forever the outcast amongst the cool kids. The whispers and stares. I had done nothing wrong, yet everyone was looking at me like I was an outcast. It hurt, more than you can imagine, having everyone you've built work relationships with for two years turn against you. Why? I couldn't find the answer, so I sucked up my pride and did as she asked with a smile.

I started to get emails from her, up to fifty daily and I was expected to keep up with all of them. Each one became more and more condescending than the last. I would send out a report to my co-workers, and they would send her the email instead of responding to me. I didn't know why, the email was nothing to report back to her, just the standings that were asked for. In return, I would get an email from her telling me to "be clear and polite." I was baffled. The emails I sent were very direct, concise and to the point. There wasn't any room for attitude in the information I relayed. Not only that, but all of my hard work and numbers would get ignored or looked over. I would have the best numbers on the team and get no recognition aside from a sneer look or whispering behind my back. Finally, I decided that enough was enough. I could play the game, too. I began to ignore my co-workers because apparently, they were just as bad as she was. Instead of being on the "Love Lisa" bandwagon, they quickly jumped on the "Hate Lisa" train without any reasoning of their own. They didn't care that she was hateful, conniving, and a bully; they just tagged along. Apparently, integrity was a lost value and I became very short with her. I would answer her questions with zero inflection. I inserted myself into a different group of people around me and we had a good time laughing and conversing.

My response to her harassment killed her because she thought isolating me would make me quit. As I continued talking with my new group, she continued to find ways to make me feel less than worthy. I had to continue to remind myself why I was there in the first place. I needed the job. I felt lost, defeated and utterly confused. How do you fix something when you don't know what you did to cause it in the first place? I wanted to give up, deal with the loss of a job, and start over somewhere else. These were the thoughts going through my head as I packed up my desk. I just couldn't deal with the condescending whispers, the looks of distaste, and the feeling of being completely isolated. I had to spend forty hours a week in a place of constant bullying. One day, I decided I'd had enough. My desk was packed and I knew I wasn't coming back. *However,* I felt God telling me to hang on a little bit longer, telling me He had a plan for me and I had to be patient.

Unfortunately, I was at my breaking point and I felt that if I had to take any more of her nonsense, I was going to seriously snap! I told God, "If you really want me to come back tomorrow, I'll be back. Just in case, I'm going to take all of my belongings with me anyway." God is almighty, all the time, and you just don't tell Him no. So there I was the next day, right back in hell's kitchen (at my desk).

Things continued to get worse. It had gotten to the point

where I couldn't stand getting up in the morning. I couldn't deal with the environment or this woman who had nothing better to do than humiliate and tear me down any chance she got. I was stripped to the core and felt stressed beyond belief. Something had to give. Knowing that I couldn't take it any longer, I began to search for a new job. As God favored me, I found one.

I listen to Marvin Sapp a lot, and I was reminded of the words of his song: *"I started dancing, I started singing."* Yes, honey, I was dancing and singing because I knew God favored me. It was such a beautiful moment. It was like the heavenly choir pulled up a shade and sang, *"Ahhh."* Yes, it felt just like that. I proudly handed them my resignation letter and I was finally free.

Soon after, I settled into my new position. Everything was great and the people were incredibly nice. I liked it there, but I was getting bored and needed more. A year into this new job, I started thinking about what else I could do well. I didn't want more interviews or to start over at another company. I wanted to work for myself. I needed to find my purpose because surely, this wasn't it. And KABOOM, it hit me. In the words of Marcus D. Reilly of the *Yolanda Adams Morning Show,* "God gave me a revelation." I had begun writing a year prior. It started with a beautiful poem entitled "God, the Silent Force"; everyone loved it. I wrote more to see if I could actually complete a novel. I think I wrote half of my book within six months. Apparently I possess an imaginative and unconventional way of thinking, which loads me up with creativity.

Going through that painful period at work led me to finding my true destiny, and it wasn't sitting behind some desk or going on another interview. I realized that getting a job, staying for two to three years, and then finding another job was showing me that I was unhappy and dissatisfied with what I was doing in life which was working for other people without a purpose. I needed something new and different, something to feed my curiosity, something to feed my creativity. Who would've known? I discovered that I had a purpose and finally, I figured out what it was.

God has gifts for us all, but the devil will sometimes make you doubt your gifts.

Looking back, I think I had Middle Child Syndrome. I've since realized that cleverness, creativity and imagination were already hidden parts of my soul. I wrote my book, *The Urban Panic* and I started a business with my husband named Poetry Pillows and Artistic Creations. Knowing my purpose put me in a better position and now I can create a legacy for my kids, which is a great feeling.

Sometimes, we already know what we're capable of, but we fail to execute.

Stop saying "I can't" and begin saying "I will." Stop saying I will, knowing you really aren't going to try. Stop being afraid to BEGIN, and start discovering what's truly yours. You must adopt an attitude of *"I may not know where I'm going, and I don't care where I've been, but it's up to me to find out what I can really do."* Start now!

Through my story, I hope you'll be inspired to reach past your obstacles and financial woes. Realize that you don't need money to have a dream; you don't even need money to begin working towards your dream. Let hope, faith and tenacity be your course of action. *You never know what you can achieve unless you take the first step.*

Now go get those blessings!

Lisa

About Lisa

Lisa L. Feggans-Odom is a talented writer, entrepreneur and native of Philadelphia, PA. Naturally artistic and creative, she began writing her debut novel *The Urban Panic* after being inspired by a poem she wrote about strangers and missing children. The story is set in a neighborhood very close to where Lisa grew up and sheds light on the dangers in our communities.

When not writing or hanging out with her husband, Tony and their two children, you can find Lisa taking pictures or creating new ideas for her company **Poetry Pillows and Artistic Creations**, an e-commerce store offering unique poetry pillows for home interior design and special gifts.

To learn more, visit
www.LisaLFeggans.com

8

MAXINE BIGBY CUNNINGHAM

Lifetime Mourning – A Healing Path

*"At its root, courage is about the core of our being -
our heart and spirit."*

S niff. Sniff. Sniff.
Something foul was in the air.
Hmmm.
What was that odor?

Nothing looked different.
Nothing looked strange.
Nothing looked out of order.
Nothing looked wrong... and yet, something was not right.

Eyes flittered, searching for the odor's source.
Ears widened, hearing only a deafening silence.
Guts grumbled, rising bile warning of wretched finding.
Tongues stilled, folks scared to even whisper.

The game could not continue.
By process of elimination,
Noses leading the way.
Feet moved up the stairs towards the reek of decaying meat.

No response to banging fists on the door.
No reply to pleading voices from outside the door.
No answer to the ringing telephone on the other side of the door.
No lessening of the stench, overwhelming at the door.

Bones stiffened.
Hearts skipped beats.
Breathing became labored.
Minds resisted imaginings...What lay behind the closed door?

Death.

Departure
So that the families of their roots could see the twins,
Mama carried us back home from Ohio to South Carolina.
Daddy remained behind. I am told that he didn't want us
to leave, but Mama insisted that our trip would be a gift,
granting Daddy time and space to prepare for final exams,
which would lead to the conferring of a Master's Degree
from Case Western Reserve University. Already, he was
the first in our family to receive a degree from an
institution of higher education located outside of the
South. Another degree would be the ticket to a better job—
perhaps becoming a college professor and a bigger home,
one with at least two bedrooms. As the three of us were
leaving, Daddy hugged me tightly, saying he would see me
when the three of us returned. My daddy lied.

Gone! I couldn't find them . . . neither Mama nor Daddy.

Was this a game of Hide and Seek? Games are fun; this
was not fun – no giggling laughter, no gleeful shouts of, "I
found you," no end to the searching.

Daddy's death remains shrouded in mystery. The discovery

occurred on a stifling hot day in late August. The heat, plus the two days that had expired, explained the stench and the rapid body decay. Autopsy reports, medical records, government papers, personal letters, journal entries, news clippings, family recollections, rampant rumors, and "what Mama said" collectively are inconsistent and incomplete. The exceptions are these two facts: (1) The death was tragic, and (2) The cause of death was so convoluted that proffered explanations were like the tip of an iceberg several miles deep.

My twin and I remember loud whispers, unwanted strangers, sideward glances, frequent admonishments not to bother Mama, and a growing concern that someone had stolen our daddy. We were 18 months old, much too young for learning, not to mention understanding the meaning of the end of life. They say we embodied Daddy: hazel-colored eyes, inquisitive by nature, always asking questions, the "red-boned" undertone of our skin, and the inclination to solve the problems of others.

When Daddy died, we also lost Mama. At barely thirty, she was a young and beautiful woman, too young to bear the name widow. And she changed. She lost weight. Her smile disappeared. Her eyes hollowed. Her touch was lifeless. When physically in our midst, her mind seemed to be elsewhere. Perhaps because Mama never saw the dead body, she never let our daddy die. Perhaps when she looked at her twin daughters, the life she mourned was resurrected. She said that everything would be okay. My mama lied.

Coping – Shame and blame. Mama said Daddy wouldn't have died had she not been away. There is supporting evidence that this really may be true. We have the letter

Daddy wrote, asking Mama to return home because he missed her. We have the testimony of my nearly centenarian aunt who said that Daddy had recently placed a telephone call to South Carolina in order to say how much he missed us and hoped we would hurry back.

For a half century, no one could have convinced me that my unexpected birth, as the younger of identical twins, did not cause stress that was just too much for Daddy to bear. A full-time employee, full-time student, and primary wage earner, he carried a very heavy load. I have the written accounts in a bound composition book, a journal of sorts where Daddy described his call to the hospital to inquire about his wife. He wrote that he was so confounded to learn he was the father of two daughters that he placed the phone in its cradle and directly finished off a bottle of wine. The baby expenses would now double. Apparently, Daddy was a detailed record keeper and recorded the family's biweekly budget as well. He noted a credit union loan for the purchase of a baby stroller.

The unanswered and inexplicable circumstances surrounding Daddy's death made coping very difficult. Was the death an accident? Suicide? Homicide? Result of an evening of alcoholic binging? Manifestation of a depressive episode? Consequence of a post-traumatic stress disorder? We were told there were two death notices. The first listed cause of death as "unknown." That conclusion was changed. Mama said that after an autopsy had been performed, the death certificate was amended and read cerebral hemorrhage. After Mama's death nearly 40 years later, we found, among her papers, an autopsy report and the second death certificate that listed cause of death. The typed words were something unexpected. The certificate read alcohol poisoning. She had closely held a big secret.

Because saying that my daddy was dead elicited such looks of pity by grade school, my twin and I no longer attached "dead" to his occupation or anything else. We started using a grown-up word, saying our daddy was "deceased." Our friends didn't know what we were talking about, and adults quickly changed the subject. Either way, we avoided the discussion of death.

Struggling to survive – Relocation. During the Great Northern Migration of the 1940s and 1950s, my daddy's family migrated from South Carolina to the Midwest, settling in the states of Michigan, Illinois and Ohio. This move was, in a sense, a flight to safety and protection from a threatened lynching of my great-grandfather, a Black Cherokee. On the other hand, Mama's family traveled to the Mid-Atlantic area, seeking jobs that would pay more than what sharecroppers took home. Her family settled in New York, Maryland and Washington, D.C. Homeless, widowed and without critical support, Mama moved us to D.C. and we doubled up in the house of her older sister and her sister's family.

Making a way out of no way – Role shifts. Initially, Mama had no inheritance and no income. Two essentials were a revenue source and someone to look after her babies. Holding a Bachelor's Degree in elementary education and possessing experience in both South Carolina and Ohio, Mama came up with a plan. She needed the freedom to travel to Ohio on probate business and to make arrangements for benefits of deceased war veterans. Solution: Mama hired her sister, a domestic worker, to care for the twins and her sister's own four children. When Mama bought a house of her own, the new house was within walking distance to her sister's house.

The twins' roles also changed. We went into a protective mode. Desperate to hold onto our mother, we assumed parental roles. The older twin appointed herself as *Security Guard*—keeping everyone happy, regardless of any personal cost. What did this look like? She seldom argued, just did what she was told and what she believed would please Mama. Of the two daughters, she was more acquiescent and obedient. The younger twin appointed herself as *Man of the House*. Rebellious at times, she told even grown folks what to do. "Auntie, smoking is bad. My daddy did not smoke." "Mama, don't dress up and go out. You stay home with us." The twins feared that their mother, too, might abandon them through death. Mama, consciously or not, allowed the role reversals.

Mindset adjustment – Reframing. *Reframing is a process of changing how a concept is presented so that it keeps its basic meaning but is easier to support resolution efforts.* In addition to facilitating conflict resolution in a business environment, reframing supports healing of emotional wounds. An unexpected death of a young man, who was a devoted husband, father, church leader, and son with a promising future before him, was given meaning beyond that of a tragedy. Deceased? Without question. Dead? No way!

These statements are not a contradiction. It depends on how you look at it. First, Daddy was visibly and audibly present. Everyone said that the twins looked "just like their daddy," and as they grew, sounded like him, too. A tape sent during the war was frequently played on a reeling tape recorder. In nearly every room was Daddy's picture—hung on the wall, atop the piano, or standing on a table's top. Second, Daddy's name was heard every single day. He had given the smaller sibling Mama's name; the younger sibling, he gave the feminine version of his own.

Third, Daddy remained a provider. Money from the insurance and veteran's benefits paid for the house's down payment, summer trips back home to South Carolina, piano lessons, health insurance, educational excursions, and college tuition.

Turning trauma into triumph

Trauma wounds. Trauma scars. Trauma triggers resentment, anger, confusion, sadness, mistrust, loneliness, blame, shame, pain, and fear. Healthy responses grow out of self-awareness, acknowledging our experiences and shaping these experiences in developing a vibrant life characterized by optimal emotional wellness.

Triumphing over trauma looked like this for us:

- The twins and Mama, all three, earned their Master's Degrees.

- My first job after college was as a Relocation Specialist.

- My daddy was an aspiring college professor and my sister received a doctorate degree and retired as an adjunct university instructor.

- Mama's standards for behavior, service, and education had but one criteria: "What would Daddy expect?"

- My twin and I have family pictures hanging on our walls, gracing our pianos, and standing on tabletops.

- Rebounding after mistakes or failures seemed the only option for Daddy's girls.

- The twins' process of healing includes writing, an

activity of the mind, body, and spirit. The older wrote *We, Too, Honor You* for a reception at which Mama received special recognition by her church. Many of her journal entries were about the subject, Daddy. The other twin wrote a poem, *Hold On*, in honor of Mama; she also penned a letter entitled *M ssing You* in honor of Daddy.

- Any time may be the last time, so my family gets together a lot. We pray, eat and sing. We talk and celebrate our children. We cry, laugh, and as we depart, we always say, "Love you."

Healing Lessons

Childhood trauma affects a woman for a lifetime. The impacts of trauma are likely conscious and unconscious, visible to the eye, but unseen by a casual observer—emotional as well as physical. However, the journey need not be characterized by a never-ending suffering. We can choose a different route, *a healing path*:

- Denial is not a healing strategy. Healing is a process that is sometimes painful.

- Healing relationships, with the living and the dead, is a *s- l- o- w* walk. Practice is required.

- Journeying on a healing path includes risk-taking, strength-training, and aerobic exercise—literally and figuratively speaking. Traveling on a healing path builds resilience, develops self-love, and produces grace and mercy.

As we sojourn along the healing path, we are compelled to let go of stuff and create room for new possibilities. Honing these survival skills sustain women in fulfilling our purposes and reaching our God-ordained destiny.

It's time for you to walk!

Maxine

About Maxine

Maxine Bigby Cunningham is the founder of Empowered Walking Enterprise/ Ministries, LLC and the creator of **"The Empowered Walking Steps to Wellness,"** a proprietary system for overcoming impediments to mental and emotional wellbeing. As a direct result of her services and products, individuals experiencing a loss, mental disorder or emotional crisis receive novel tools and "inside-out" strategies for optimal well-being for both themselves and others. She addresses the hard question, "What must I do to be well in body, mind and spirit?"

Maxine lives with a serious chronic mental illness, often with nearly deadly somatic manifestations. While recovering from a major episode, Maxine chronicled her 11-year journey to recovery in her self-published memoir and wellness guide, ***Power Walking, A Journey to Wholeness***. This is a story of healing brokenness of the body, mind and spirit which sets forth The Empowered Walking Steps to Wellness. Her articles appear in personal growth, mental health and Christian living publications.

To learn more, visit
www.MentalEmotionalWellness.com

9

A. NAFISA COOPER

Misled by a Hidden Truth

We all remember the terrible crack cocaine epidemic that reigned the streets of the inner cities back in the 80s and 90s. Most people in my neighborhood either used the drug or sold it. The daily ritual of passing through street corners filled with drug dealers, the neighborhood crack users, and the mix of normal folk made you oblivious to the dangers we actually lived under.

The devastation was watching my loved ones turn into what we called "crack zombies," selling their souls to the devil himself for five dollars a hit. They were dismal vessels with very little hope of survival. It hurt like hell to watch.

After many years of watching the desolation within our inner-city communities, the destruction of families and friends, the untimely deaths of so many youth, the resurgence of rehabilitative services and nationwide community rebuilding efforts was the relief and breath of fresh air many of us activists turned to and needed. I became an advocate, the voice for the underdog. Wherever there was a need for change, I wanted to find a solution.

The socially and economically disadvantaged individuals and families within our community were who I cared most about. The social ills that plagued our communities became part of an agenda to make a difference where it really mattered.

The passion and drive I had to make a difference existed mostly due to the children growing up in the area; they didn't deserve to be subjected to that way of life. As a mother, striving to give my children more out of life than I had, the obligation to do all I could just felt right. This was my calling. As a woman raised in a family of strong women, I knew that showing my children anything different wasn't acceptable. By the grace and mercy of the Creator, the mission and vision to create a bridge of communication, self-awareness, and the desire to empower those deemed powerless, came with ease. My conversion back to Islam and my strong moral compass was the foundation I needed to address the most taboo topics affecting our community.

I was just as active in my religious community as the community I lived in. As a single mother raising four children without the security and companionship of a good mate and role model, marriage was next on my agenda. After many prospects, the decision to marry relied mostly on my intended's love for the religion, his humility, and his desire for a family. He didn't have much, but I saw enough within him that he became sufficient. The familial roles and family hierarchy in Islam were clear to us; the spiritual connection would be the bond we based our marriage on.

The courtship was short and sweet. I was greeted daily on my way in from work and surprised with a gift or trinket. This man made me smile. He'd wink at me and I'd melt. He showed me that real men still existed and that chivalry wasn't dead. I loved him for making me feel his love.

One rainy day as I returned home from work, in front of strangers and God, he met me in the pouring rain, got down on one knee and presented me with the most beautiful ring. I cried from the sentiment. As I stood there, soaking wet, nothing else existed. It was only us.

I fell in love hard and fast; there was nothing keeping me from being his everything. I was caught up in all that was him, and I loved it. Not only did I believe that what I had was the realest love, I believed that he was my soul mate.

I thought I knew everything about him, no secrets. I asked every question I could think of and yet, I was misled…

Misled and blinded by love. This was devastation to the 10th power. *How could I have found myself madly in love with a crack addict?* Was I so blindsided by love that the signs became oblivious to me? I found myself in a daily routine of missing money and consistent lying. I was hurt beyond words and scared. Scared that I had involved my children into the very thing I was trying to prevent. Behaviors of abuse and desperation became prevalent, making me feel as if this wasn't the person who touched my heart so deeply. Still, I sat along the sidelines in a marriage I believed was doomed to fail. I was ready to leave, but I had to give him the benefit of the doubt. When I first confronted him with my suspicions, he lied. Between the secrets and the lies, I decided this was all on him. He hurt me. He broke our trust, our friendship. He did this to me! The more I convinced myself this was something he should deal with on his own, the harder he fought to stay. He used my love, claiming that I could make him better. His self-loathing, disappearing acts, and abusive words cut through my heart like a knife. This was unlike any pain I had ever known. I was angry and felt used.

It just wasn't fair. There were other prospects with more money, more clout, who believed I could learn to love and be a good wife. After all, they were pursuing me. I was driving a nice car, had my own home, good health, a great job, and I was both God-fearing and a really good catch. Furthermore, I was pursuing my Bachelor's degree in Communications and running a successful nonprofit business.

This situation wasn't for me, but I had to remind myself that I was his wife. I was angry and emotional, finding it difficult to understand how I was faithful, trusting and did everything right. I wanted and needed my knight in shining armor! And he was not it by a long shot!

My husband insisted so many times that things would get better and that he just needed to work this out; I started believing this was just a ploy to keep a roof over his head whenever he'd come home from his runs. I was in a loveless, sexless marriage.

During this unfortunate turn in my life, I began to question my prowess as a woman. I needed the comfort of my man to keep the kitty alive and purring. My fear of my Lord kept me from seeking comfort in the arms of another, so I dealt with being put on the back burner in my marriage. Although I hurt deeply, I didn't leave. Somewhere in his words and requests to be patient, I found myself wanting to believe him.

I began to lose all the things I'd worked so hard for. I struggled to pay bills—literally living from paycheck to paycheck, barely making it. There were days when a decent meal was a luxury. Times became harder than I'd ever known. My spirit was broken and my outlook on life was bleak. I just wasn't the person I'd been. My unyielding attitude and desire to change the ills around us was now more personal than it'd ever been. *Where do you get help when you're the one helping everybody?* My issues were looked at as minimal because I was the sister known to march through the trenches to fight for the rights of the weak and disadvantaged. But it was me and there was no one to help, no one to step up and help me see the light at the end of the tunnel.

This was a major shock to my system, specifically when I sought help and empathy from those I believed were true friends. It saddened me to find that very few people in my circle genuinely gave a damn about me and what I was going through. I was shown that I was a means to an end for so many. Here I was, no real friends, a hopeless marriage, unhappy and struggling to make it day to day. The deterioration of my health and the failure of my business began to take its toll on me, too. Depression and sadness set in, and I found security in my bed; it was my crutch, while food became my comfort. Good sex and being in love became a memory. It was the marriage from hell.

During the time, my only living parent, my father, became ill. I cared for him, then watched him lose his battle with kidney disease. His death was devastating. Now I was completely alone in the big world.

After years of struggling with my husband's addiction, a major move to another state gave us a turning point and chance at recovery. I still struggled with questioning and believing in him, yet I found a way to be a supportive wife.

I gave him what no other woman had ever given him, including his mother: I didn't abandon him. It takes a lot to get through an issue of distrust in a marriage. Once it's shaken, the battle to get it back is all uphill. Still angry and hurt by the deception I was fed, I was now resentful. The roles in our marriage had changed. I was now bringing in more money. I was the one who always found a way to make it through, and the struggle was difficult. My husband was finally many years clean, and I figured we could enjoy our marriage. *But how do you get back everything that was lost when you're starting from nothing?* I didn't say I loved him, I offered no affection, and kisses and sex were still a thing of the past.

My body was changing and my sex appeal had turned into frumpiness. Walking past the mirrors in our house scared me. I no longer recognized myself. The weight gain was one thing, then came the high blood pressure and kidney disease, along with being an insulin-dependent diabetic.

As time went on, I started having trouble walking, a severe vitamin deficiency caused me chronic pain, and I started losing my sight. All of a sudden, the things I'd taken for granted became a chore. The simplest things, like tying my shoes, showering, and dressing myself had become difficult.

No longer able to walk without the assistance of a cane or walker, unable to read because of my distorted vision, not being able to hold anything steadily or dial a phone because of tremors in my hands, I was literally a shell of the woman I once was. I barely remembered what it was like to feel a love so deep with a man and have so much hope for our future. I was still angry, resentful and afraid I'd been given a death sentence. I still felt alone. No one should have to die alone. No one should be in a situation without the support of their spouse or family. Where would I turn for help and how could I live without anything to live for? This became my reality. I ultimately had to have surgery. I remember lying on the hospital bed, tears rolling down my face, worried I was dying and sad at the absence of the people who claimed to have love for me. As the tears continued flowing, I cried out to my Lord, pleading with Him to please have mercy on me and help me.

I thought of my favorite Bible story about the prophet Job and how, through all his trials, he never lost sight of his purpose, nor did he allow his faith to be shaken. He lost everything: his family, his health, wealth and social status. Although I could never be compared to Job, I found his resilience and conviction inspirational. I also found that just for the asking, all he lost was restored. God, with His infinite mercy, shows us how taking away what we have is nothing to Him. He also shows that His promises are true. He wants us to call on Him and He'll respond. God is sufficient for us. Job showed us that his worship and covenant with God was the most important thing in his life, and that nothing or no one would ever come close.

It was then that it dawned on me...I was never alone. *This was a test, not an admonishment.* All the support and love I looked for was given to me in ways I couldn't see. I didn't need anyone or anything except what was there all along. I gave into selfish desires that created a world of misery and distrust when all I should've done was put my trust and faith in my higher power.

Today, I've accepted my illness and how much my life has changed. I'm humbled and grateful for what I've learned.

I'm no longer angry or playing the blame game. I've grown spiritually and my outlook is no longer grim. I live with hope daily. I'm moved by my ability and gift that the Lord allows me to use for my testimony as a platform and inspiration for others. What I thought was one of the worst times of my life was actually my difficulty leading to my ease. I could never appreciate the ease of how I'm living without going through the difficult time.

My husband is now my rock; he upholds me in ways I never thought possible. He's become the man I need even more than the man I fell so deeply in love with. There's nothing I'd change about who he is or where he came from. His love for me has grown as mine for him. When he winks at me from across the room, I still melt inside like a school girl. Our bond is stronger than I ever believed possible. There is nothing we can't overcome together. We've both learned that marriage isn't something to give up on, that *honesty and open communication are the keys to building unbreakable trust.*

The institution of marriage in the sight of God is greater than most of us will admit. Marriage takes work. There are hardships, but starting with a foundation of faith is what makes it last. I still cry, but now they're tears of gratitude. With all we've endured, we're blessed to understand that the troubling times were well worth the ease the Lord has given us.

Giving up is easy, but not always the right thing to do, regardless of how grim things may be. In all we go through, there's a lesson to be learned. And when faith is your starting point, giving in to the expectations of others or making decisions based on selfish reasoning shouldn't be an option. Taking accountability for your actions and decisions should be done without regret.

Don't just give in, give it to God. With Him, all things are possible.

Nafisa

About Nafisa

Rest In Paradise

On January 11, 2014, one month after the release of this book, Nafisa passed away due to kidney complications at the early age of 43. She will always be remembered for her beautiful smile, selfless heart and as a vessel for others in the struggle of life. She is greatly missed!

Born and raised in Philadelphia, PA, Antoinette Nafisa Cooper-Micheaux was an African-American Muslim, Victims' Advocate, Nonprofit Consultant, Professional Writer and Community Activist. A devoted wife and mother of four children and six grandchildren, she was best known in both the Muslim and secular communities for her activism and years of service to victims of abuse and the socially and economically disadvantaged.

She was the founder of **Sista2Sista Inc.**, the first organization in the City of Philadelphia to address domestic violence in the Muslim community. Sista2Sista Inc. successfully ran the first resource and referral hotline for Abused Muslim Women across the country, helping over 2,000 victims and counting.

To learn more, visit
www.WeAreBentNotBroken.com

10

ARADIA KNIGHT

Lost and Found

*Have you ever been so down on your luck that you had to
laugh at your own pain?*

My best friend lost her apartment and her kids to
Child Protective Services. Both of us were on the
streets without a place to live. We ended up
getting a room with two beds at the Motel 6 for the night.
The next morning, we walked next door to IHOP for
breakfast. When we got back to the room, it was locked. We
had already taken all of our stuff back to the car before
heading to breakfast, but we still needed to take a shower.
We both walked silently to the car and stood there for a
moment looking at each other with straight faces from
opposite sides of my car and suddenly started laughing at
the realization that we were both homeless and had
absolutely *nowhere* to go! It was then I knew that I
had to get my life back on track.

I had, what most would consider, a pretty great childhood.
I had a great upbringing. I was a military brat, Navy and
lived with both of my parents. We didn't live the Cosby life,
but I *never* saw that we struggled. Whatever my sister and I
needed, our parents always pulled through to get it.

A few years after high school, I married a military man and we began having babies of our own. He wanted the archetypical marriage where he provided while I took care of the children and the household. That just wasn't my thing. I had goals and ambitions. I couldn't just sit at home while he went to work every day. I was attending college, running a new business, raising my children, and holding down the fort when my husband was called on deployment during 9/11 (when the towers went down). During this time, my husband cheated often. As much as I wanted to leave him, I didn't; I couldn't. I stayed because I was provided for, and felt that I had to settle for the treatment I was given. After many years of infidelity and lies, things finally came to a head when I found out he was sleeping with some of my closest friends. I despised him. My babies were young and I was tired of them being subjected to the turmoil of seeing us fuss and fight about his philandering ways.

Enough was enough. We had to separate. He moved out to stay on post while I stayed in the house that he and I leased together. Ultimately, we ended up divorcing. When he left, things began to fall apart. Because our lifestyle was so extravagant, my income alone wasn't enough to take care of myself—let alone the basic needs of my children. He was deployed overseas again and my kids and I were left to fend for ourselves. Worse than that, he didn't care. That fact alone made me despise him even more. He was very materialistic; 'things' were more important to him than seeing that his children had a stable roof over their heads and were cared for. I was working, but it just wasn't enough. I knew that eventually things would turn around. I knew that I would come out this situation and would show him that I didn't need him after all.

In difficult times like these, the first place you usually turn to is your family. My pride kept me from turning to my father. I didn't want him to see me like this. My mother, on the other hand, was cold and callous, full of negativity. She allowed my kids to live in her home with her and my sister, for which I'm thankful, but she kept me out. I'd sleep outside of her apartment complex, in my car. In the morning, I would get up and get my kids ready for school. My kids and I would shower and leave for the day until the evening when I had to leave. The area my mother lived in wasn't safe and often had a lot of drug activity going on. I knew something had to give after a gang fight broke out in my mother's neighborhood. I drove to my old elementary school a few blocks down and slept in the parking lot there. The school parking lot became my newest place to squat. Nobody was around and I felt a little safer there because I knew the neighborhood.

In between my kids being at my mother's house and me sleeping in the car, I made the best out of my days and found a place to stay, though I knew I couldn't afford it. Although my business was doing okay, I had bills and other expenses for the business that I needed to take care of and wasn't managing the money as best as I could have. I'd get a place and then realize that I'd probably only be able to stay there for two to three months before it was over. Squatting now became how we got by.

A year later, I was diagnosed with pulmonary embolism and I had to call my kids' father to come take care of them. I stayed in the hospital for a while and when I was released, I had been evicted. Here I was homeless again, sleeping in my car or wherever I could. I had friends who let me into their houses from time to time to freshen up and take a shower, but I knew tho se friendships wouldn't last long. At one time, I had helped these people in some form. When they didn't have food or money, I'd give it to them, freely—even to the point of sacrificing my own bills. When it was time to pay their bills, I'd help them with that, too. Now, I was the one in trouble and everyone turned a blind eye. As a last resort, I called my mother. This time, she let me stay with her, though she acted funny about it. I bit the bullet and stayed anyway.

Right away, the living situation wasn't good. My mother was smoking weed a lot and my sister was on drugs. This was definitely not the life I had envisioned for myself. While living in this situation and seeing the dealers come in and out the house selling drugs to my mother and sister, I could only remember thinking to myself that I needed to get rid of a lot of people in my life; my mother and sister were the first ones to go. I still had employees working for me in my business at the time, but some of them needed to be let go. I knew it was time for me to get stable and get my children and my life back on track, but eventually, the situation had gotten to me—to the point where I didn't give a damn anymore and considered suicide. There was a time I took so many pills that I ended up in the hospital. They pumped my stomach and gave me some black stuff to drink that looked and tasted like tar, but tasted sweet compared to all the pills I had taken. I wanted to take myself out. Truthfully, I felt no one cared about me or what I was going through. I was grateful for a roof over my head, even if it was at the hospital. They wanted to keep me there overnight, so that meant that I was getting food, too. My hospital stay fortified the idea of me doing crazy things to myself, but I had kids to think about—kids who needed me and had nothing to do with any of this. It was my job to pick myself up and bounce back.

I had to choose to change my mindset and my behavior, and that's exactly what I did.

Eventually, I did get back on my feet and into a stable place, and my business started booming. My oldest and youngest children were back with me and my other children were still living with their dad until I had fully recovered from my hospitalization. As time passed with things going good, a friend of mine, who was in the army, asked me if I could take care of her son in Texas while she deployed overseas. I wasn't living in Texas nor was she yet stationed in Texas yet, but I told her I would and to let me know when the move was definite. Months passed, she finally got back to me, but instead of getting stationed in Texas, she was getting stationed in Georgia. Talking to her previously about her possible move to Texas planted a seed in my mind. I heard people talk about living in Texas all the time. My best friend, who I was homeless with in the past, had moved to Houston, got settled and was on her feet doing great things.

I decided to take a leap of faith, hoping and praying that when it was my turn to leave for Texas, the blessings that were flowing in her life would flow into mine.

I was so excited that I got up and left. I knew it was time for me to leave the state. I couldn't take it anymore. I wasn't progressing, it was too expensive, I had it all then lost it all, then lost some more, and couldn't fully get back on my feet. I really just wanted to start over and get to a place where my health was great and I had all five of my children with me. *I knew that if I wanted something for myself, I had to get out there and make it happen. I had stood in my own way for many years,* but I got out of my own way and went to get everything that I wanted and needed—for not only myself, but for my children as well.

I told my family that I was moving to Texas. A couple of days after that, I called a trucking company. Keep in mind, I was still broke, but I called them anyway and scheduled a time for them to pack up my things and move them to Texas, with still no place to go. The trucking company quoted me $700 and I asked them if they could come that same week. Now I'm thinking to myself, *"Where am I going to get this money from? And what am I going to tell my clients, because I can't take all of them with me. Go figure! Here I am doing well with my business—helping other businesses keep their financial houses in order—and I'm broke."* I made the appointment for the trucking company to come and sent out an email blast to all of my clients, letting them know that I was leaving. From that email, I was only able to keep two of my clients. Between the both of them, I was only earning about $600 a month, but I figured that would be enough to hold me. Then I went to an agency and told them I was moving and needed assistance. They looked at my income and gave me a one-time payment of $1,500 to do whatever I needed to do. Now, I had a total of $2,100 in my pocket. That would *definitely* work!

Next up was finding a place to live. I got on Craigslist and I lucked up with a very nice lady who was renting her home out. I sealed the deal with her and signed the lease agreement via fax, never meeting the woman. I let her know the trucking company would be leaving the next day and that I would be at the house in the next four or five days. She told me she would leave the keys under the plant by the front door. When we were ready to leave and were saying our goodbyes, my mother was negative, telling me that she knew I was going to fail in Texas. Though it hurt,

I let it go, finally accepting that this was just who she was.

The following day, Washington State was seeing my back and I vowed to never step foot there again. Our new home was in Killeen. I looked up potential friends on BlackPlanet.com and met a few married women. I figured *if* and *when* I did get married, I wanted to have married friends. I let them know I was coming to town and was interested in meeting new people. One of the women I had only known for a short time was at my new home when I pulled up, waiting to greet me and my kids on our doorstep. I knew we wouldn't have electricity when we arrived, but my two children and I were willing to take the chance of living there without power. Fortunately, the young lady took my kids and me back to her home to stay with her and her family. We crashed there for a week. She was truly heaven-sent.

After settling into my house for a few months, I met a guy and we ended up getting pretty serious, so serious that my kids and I moved in with him. Then we got married. He was also in the military and took care of everything. He was very patient with me. I had slowed down with my business and he encouraged me to take some time to figure out what I really wanted to do and to let him know when I knew. In 2010, I decided to take a year off from my business.

After that year, I knew it was time to get back to doing what I loved. Not only was I doing personal bookkeeping for my household, soldiers started asking me to create budgets for their households. I had always envisioned my bookkeeping business being everywhere, but had to figure out how I was going to get there. I went back to the table on my business that had been sitting dormant for a year. I wanted to be able to reach everybody worldwide, so I knew my business needed to be online. We started the branding process. At times I would give up, but then remind myself that I needed to *trust the process.*

My husband, even after he and I called our marriage quits, invested in me and my dream of seeing Aidara, Inc.™ connect with businesses worldwide, helping and assisting in getting their financial houses in order. I think about how he never turned his back on me during this process. Regardless of how things turned out between us, at the end of the day, he's the reason why I am where I am. If he hadn't come into my life and provided the stability my kids and I needed, I would still be lost.

After my business took off, everything started to fall into place. To date, I'm a homeowner and I have all five of my children with me. I just sent my oldest daughter off to college at an HBCU and am getting reacquainted with the three that had been estranged from me through all the craziness.

When you are weathering the storm, it can be difficult to see how you're going to make it through.

Keep pushing through and trust the process. I'm a firm believer of things getting really bad before they get really good.

Don't get comfortable and don't quit. Strive for the better and be a fighter. You deserve the best, so don't stop until you get it. Remember, there's always a blessing in the storm. If you keep pressing ahead, you will reap the reward.

Be aggressive. You have to be aggressive in order to stand up and meet your ambitions...just like I did.

Aradia

About Aradia

Aradia Knight is the Founder and President of Aidara, Inc.™ She is a business visionary, a dynamic community leader, and a popular instructor. In 2013, Aradia was honored by the Forbes-ranked leadership company, Stiletto Woman Media as *Entrepreneur of the Year* for Business and Consulting Services at the SWIBA Awards in Atlanta, GA. Aradia's passion for her business is equaled by her dedication to service, and her generous spirit touches many lives. She participates in many local initiatives that include youth programs, empowerment programs and mentorships.

To learn more, visit
www.About.me/AradiaKnight

11

TRINISA M. PITTS

Unlived Promises:
He Loves Me, He Loves Me Not – I Deserve!

When asked to participate in this collaboration, I had stability in my life. Well, at least that's what I thought. Everything is going well with me, I'm learning to live after the pain. I'm following God's plan for my life and everything is looking up. I'm fifteen years drug-free, two years and ten months alcohol-free, and my depressive state of mind is nowhere near where it was. I invited God into my life and He showed me a peace like I have never known, but there was still something hindering me. I had the weight of the world on my shoulders in the form of a man. I knew that if I could just let go of the baggage I was holding onto (or that was holding onto me), my heart would feel much lighter and my world would shine much brighter. It was time for me to let go and let God.

This opportunity came at just the right time in my life, when I was ready to reveal so I could heal and let go of the chains binding me. I knew my breakthrough was here; I could see the light, I was just too scared to walk toward it. Now, I'm revealing myself to you so maybe we can take this journey together. Our breakthrough is here today.

How many times have you wondered if a guy truly loved you? It hurts even more to think that he never loved you at all. This guy was my best friend, the one I went to with all my problems and secrets. After years of just hanging out and being friends, I was the one who crossed the line. Yes, it was me! If you're wondering if a man and a woman can be platonic, I say no! In my experience, feelings will be exchanged somewhere down the line.

I had no clue this guy didn't see me the same way I saw him. We exchanged money and did things for each other, but after years of us just being friends, things changed, and *I realized I was in a one-sided relationship.* He could go home to his girlfriend while I was left alone, not able to see anyone else. Right now, you may be reading this with your mouth wide open. Yes, he had a girlfriend, but in the beginning, he didn't have a child with her. He kept telling me he was going to leave her, that he wasn't happy, and that it wasn't what he wanted. All lies. "Why are you still with her then?"

Eventually, the child came, and he basically said, "I can't leave now!" So, there I was, holding on to a dream and a promise. And here I am, *thirteen years* later, still not in a committed relationship with this man. I'd tried to leave him, time and time again, and we'd end up right back in the midst of a so-called relationship after saying we were only going to be friends that time around. About two years ago, when I stopped drinking, I started seeing things for what they really were: Nothing! This man was having his cake and eating it, too. I began telling him that I was in a different place in my life—that I had stopped drinking and I was diligently seeking God for all my answers and the right way to live. I truly didn't want to be in that situation any longer.

Well, it seems the more I told him I wanted out of the relationship, the more actively he sought me out, trying to draw us closer together. Or so he wanted me to believe. I continued to pray for God to remove me from the situation. I went from wanting him around me all the time to wanting to be alone. I knew that when he left me, he was going home to her. It wasn't sitting right with me anymore and I could no longer pretend like I was okay with the situation. I hated it and I was starting to dislike myself for putting up with such foolishness. I used to pray to God, saying, "Lord, tell me, does he loves me or does he loves me not?" Each and every time I asked that question, God showed me something. I'd see him and his girlfriend at a red light or in the grocery store. There had even been times that the girlfriend overheard a conversation he and I had and she would call my phone. He was telling her, "Oh, Trinisa is just my friend. She has a boyfriend." One day, she called me and asked, "Since you have a boyfriend, why are you always talking to my man?" Since I was drunk on this particular night, about 10 years ago, I said, "I do have a boyfriend; [your man] is my boyfriend." Yes, this thing was deep. I could go on and on about different situations, but I want to tell you how I learned to let it go. *I started to realize I deserved much more than the heartache* of seeing them together and having to hear the "I'm sorry, but you knew I had a woman" spiel.

As I mentioned, I prayed that God would help me with this situation, "Lord, if it's for me, keep me in it and help me to be patient until he's out of what he claims he doesn't want." Well, because I kept going back, I thought that was God telling me that's where I should be. NOT! It was *me telling me* this is where I wanted to be.

As I continued to dig deep into the word of God, I learned

so much more about right and wrong, our sins we bear and the burdens we carry. I trusted that the Lord would eventually remove these feelings from me. Keep in mind, this was my best friend, my drinking partner, my buddy. How could God remove the loving feelings without the whole kit and caboodle? I cried; I asked God for the strength to overcome my fear of being completely without this man in my life, as a friend or a lover. I knew I deserved more than he was willing to give me and I had to find a way out, but how? Now I know that prayer really does change things. I had to give my all to God and let Him handle it. Each and every time I was weak in my flesh, God was making my mind stronger.

About two years ago, I don't recall how the conversation came about, but he said, "Trinisa, I didn't even like you like that until about a year ago." Wow! Can you imagine how I felt? The man I had been through hell and high water with just told me he didn't like me like that, after all I'd been through with him. At that particular point, it was all-or-nothing for me. I was determined to make a change in my life. I wanted out and it didn't matter how long it took. I started building a wall that he couldn't climb to get to me. Yes, I still talked to him, still let him visit. I still did things for him and he did things for me, but my mindset changed and my heart hardened. I knew it was time to truly let this situation go. I wanted revenge because I wanted to hurt him like he'd hurt me with his words. Every chance I had, I'd let him know I didn't want to be in a relationship, nor did I want to be in a friendship. I'd put him out of my house and I'd say hurtful things to him. I wanted him to see how it felt to be degraded because that's exactly how I felt. He wasn't the only man who'd hurt me, but this one was the hardest to let go of. He'd given me more than any other man had. He was my friend; at least,

I thought he was. Turns out, I really didn't know him at all. He would throw things in my face that I'd told him in secrecy. He'd ask for things back after he'd given them to me. I just couldn't believe that someone who said he loved me could hurt me in the same breath. That's not what my love was all about. I decided to use that exact situation as fuel to ignite my movement. I had to stop trying to sit in where I didn't fit in! It was time to stop living in his world of manipulation and make a world of my own.

I knew I deserved more. I'm a woman who has never asked for anything. I've done everything on my own: no public assistance or Section 8. I've always worked two jobs; I went to school and got a degree. I put both of my girls through college by myself. I own my own home, and I have a career, dreams, and goals I'm presently working towards. I stopped drinking and drugging without any programs, just by the grace of God alone, so I know there is more to me than the eyes can see. *I deserve more!*

I wanted to learn more about me as a person, not me as the lonely, desperate woman this guy tried to make me feel like. What I finally discovered was that a man doesn't complete me. I deserved more and I was destined to find it. The only thing I had to do was begin to let go. I'm still letting go. You see, this is a process and my process was beginning to write. I found a love for something other than him I could focus my attention on. The more I wrote, the more I realized that *this* was my purpose in life—not being someone's second woman or being someone's go-to person when a favor was needed. This guy used my abilities as a strong, dominant woman to his advantage and I couldn't let him continue to use me. I took all the time I spent trying to make him love and be with me and turned it into my passion to write, the gift God gave me.

When I began expressing myself through words with pen and paper, I knew it would be easy. I found an outlet for my pain and discovered that the power of the pen is miraculous. I needed to focus all my attention on God so He could strengthen me. I knew it wouldn't happen overnight. I had known this man for fifteen years and we had been together for thirteen. Every time I'd try to leave him, he would manipulate me, saying I always tried to leave when he was down.

Let me tell you how God fixed this. We often pray to God to fix *us*, but He sometimes fixes *the situation*. In this particular case, God picked him up. He's now eight months alcohol-free, has three jobs, a nice truck and is doing well. I'm proud of him and I have to admit that I do love him and want the best for him, but I shouldn't be with him. I see that God fixed it so he wouldn't have a reason to say I was leaving him at a bad time. He's gotten himself together, but my feelings have changed; we're both in different places in our lives. Even with him getting himself together in that area, he still has baggage that I'm not willing to attach myself to again. God has shown me that I'm important and that my job is not to please him or any other man. I should be treated with respect because I'm a woman. I finally realized I knew the answer all along to the question: *Does he love me or does he not?* He loved the things I could do for him, but I'm not so sure about loving me.

Where am I now? I'm a woman of God and author of *The Essence of Me: Life After the Pain.* I'm a co-author in numerous book collaborations, an independent columnist, freelance writer, poet, and motivational and inspirational speaker. I'm doing with my life what God intended. He has given me the strength I need to overcome any and all situations that aren't edifying to my soul, including my former relationship, which was killing me softly. It was eating at my heart each and every time I went back. I felt like I was caged in; I wanted to be free and I was. God has given me the courage to fly and face my fears with faith. Letting go and letting God was the most important decision I have ever made. While it may feel uncomfortable, I'm in the right place. I know the best is yet to come for me. I had to let go so God could place something else in my path. However, I'm not looking for it—I'm waiting on God. He's the only one who knows when my season will come.

From this situation, I learned that "single" *is not a dirty word nor is it a disease.* I used to think that if someone didn't see me with a man, they would think something was wrong with me. No, there isn't anything wrong with me! It's merely not my time or season for a man. If you're currently in your season of singleness, I suggest using this time to get to know who you are, whose you are, and what you're willing to let inside your heart. My goal is to find peace within myself. *We must learn to love ourselves before we give love to anyone else.* Let us not lose who we are to a man who doesn't really complement us.

I want to leave you with this advice:

* Learn to have a personal relationship with God. Learn to talk with Him and kick it with Him. He'll give you the answers you need before making any choices in your life.

* Never allow yourself to be the second woman because you deserve better. The same things you learn to accept are the same things you'll regret in the end!

- Set boundaries. Never let anyone walk all over you. When you say no, mean it! Don't let people take your kindness for weakness. You are nobody's doormat.

"Not that I speak in regards to need, for I have learned in whatever state I am in to be content!"
- **Philippians 4:11**

Trinisa

About Trinisa

Electrifying audiences and inspiring dramatic life changes, Trinisa M. Pitts helps those struggling with overwhelming challenges in life by sharing her personal testimony of overcoming addiction, abuse and heartache. She empowers her audience to embrace a life filled with forgiveness, purpose and *The Divine* by sharing the tools to fearlessly face adversity. Trinisa is a native of Syracuse, NY who started her journey of true and diligent healing several years ago when she decided to let go and let GOD guide her path. She has since authored two works, ***The Essence of Me: Life After the Pain*** and ***Trinisa's 365 Day Daily Inspirations***. She has also contributed to three other book collaborations, *Chronicles of a Walk with Christ, A Letter to My Mother: A Daughter's Perspective,* and *When Sister's Pray.*

To learn more, visit
www.TrinisaMPitts.com

12

STACY Y. WHYTE

Afflicted, But Not Crushed

It was a summer day at the office and I was looking and feeling good. I said good morning to everyone I saw before stopping to chat with my friend Natalie. We always had so much to talk about, from her charming boyfriend to her kids to her partying in her downtime. We had a good laugh over her club experience, and then, it was time to start my day.

I had created a great sales strategy based on why clients should choose the services being offered by the company I represented. Even when others were not making sales, I was at the top of the ladder. As a top performer, I always took home coveted prizes such as flat-screen TVs and Zale's jewelry. I never complained about my job—I really enjoyed going to work every single day.

A few weeks later, I went into the office, as usual, and everything was going well. I made ten sales before 2 p.m., but as I stood up from my desk, a pain shot through me, leaving me in agony from my hips to my toes. I fell flat on my back, my ankle out of alignment, my hip twisted and curved, and tears streaming down my face. I couldn't get up. I was supposed to receive my award for top performer of the month that afternoon. Instead, I ended up in a hospital bed.

I spent almost three weeks there as doctors ran test after test because I had no feeling in my legs. I couldn't use the restroom or take a shower without assistance. With the loss of my independence and privacy, I felt like my whole world had exploded into tiny pieces. After I was released from the hospital, I spent my days alone at home. The caretaker only came in for three to four hours at a time and she wasn't the friendliest person. It was like she wasn't there at all. She did what she had to do and rarely spoke to me. I was so sad that I couldn't do anything for myself because I couldn't walk, and that's when it hit me. I was disabled! I cried until my tears became the water I drank, but I pressed on because I wanted to live.

Still, that fall really set me back from where I could have been. With every day, my hopes of walking again faded even more. I had been seeing so many doctors and specialists, hoping and believing that with all their experience, they would eventually find a miracle pill that would allow me to regain movement in my legs. That never happened. Instead, pain and discomfort became my daily bread.

Visits from my friends at the office dwindled as the weeks and months went by. My neighbors assisted me with my grocery shopping and sometimes prepared meals for me. That's how I met my friend, Duane. He would visit with his daughter and check on me from time to time. He never came empty-handed, always bringing something, whether it was groceries or flowers. He always offered a treat to cheer me up and put a smile on my face. Many days, I was laughing in the presence of others, while fear and depression continued to cripple me inside. It had me wrapped up in a spider's web, but God held me together so I wouldn't lose my mind.

One day, a driver came to pick me up for my doctor's appointment and I was in so much pain I couldn't even get up to get dressed. My friend, Laura from work was spending a few weeks with me. She was calm and spoke to me in a soft tone, never rushing me or raising her voice. I kept hearing her say, "Stacy, we are going to get through this together." The driver called and spoke with Laura because he'd been waiting for a long time. On our way to the appointment, he started telling me about his mother, who had suffered terribly before passing away from a brain tumor. In that moment, I realized just how fortunate I was to be alive.

That day was filled with bad news, but something inside of me kept telling me that *I couldn't give up*. Hopelessness washed over me as the specialist told me, "You have developed a disease called reflex sympathetic dystrophy. You will never be able to walk again. We still do not know why you have no feeling in your legs."

Although I felt like giving up, I remembered my mother's words to me when I was a child, "What is too big for you is not too big for God." Laura held my hands as only a friend would, looking me in the eyes and saying, "Stacy, I've got you. God has you in the palm of His hands. This is not too big for God to handle, my friend. I will support you in whatever capacity I can." Those words reassured me that I would one day rise again.

A few weeks later, Laura and I were sitting on the sofa in the living room when the doorbell rang. To our surprise, two Jehovah's Witnesses stood there. I've always opened my heart to others, so I was curious about what they had to say. Those two women came at the right time to resurrect my hope with a message about God and His Son,

Jesus Christ, and the love they have for me. They told me about a woman who had an issue of blood and how Jesus healed her because of her faith. Later, one of the ladies said that God could also heal me, so I should *continue to believe in His promises for me because He is faithful.* It was an on-time word for that set hour and I'll be forever grateful for that moment. They exhibited such care and love toward me that I felt like God had sent them there just for me.

That day was a divine moment that shaped my life into what it is now. I started reading the Bible and learning to pray. I read the *"Our Father"* prayer in the book of Matthew twice a day until I started praying on my own. Before that, I thought the Bible was for little old and retired people, that it would bore me to death. I didn't know how to pray or what to pray for before that day. Afterward, I developed an active prayer life. As I began to commune with God, I started to notice changes in my demeanor, my attitude, my mindset, and even my health. Being disabled for almost twenty-two months had humbled me, but a relationship with God gave me joy and inner peace that I never knew existed. My friends noticed it, too. Each time they visited, they would say, "Stacy, something has changed with you. Your eyes reflect joy and happiness. What's going on?" I used the opportunity to share the Scriptures with them. Not everyone was receptive, but I kept going and growing in the word.

I had found peace by looking beyond my issues and focusing my attention on others. For example, Duane's daughter needed assistance with her schoolwork, so I tutored her. I felt so fulfilled each time we reviewed the coursework and she answered correctly. Not to mention when she brought her new and improved report card home to show me. It was certainly a season of gratification for me and I was happy I could contribute positively to someone else's success.

However, I still had moments of darkness. A few weeks later, while doing my devotion, I cried out to God for healing. I kept saying, "When will you heal me? If you are not going to heal me, just let me die because I am tired. God, I am tired, so tired." I remember throwing my Bible on the floor, demanding, "Talk to me so I know you are there and hearing me." For a while, I lay on the ground in total silence. Then I heard a voice. "Get up and walk."

I sat up, looked around, and saw no one. I took a deep breath and then laid back down. I heard it a second time, "Get up and walk." This time, it sounded like rolling thunder and I felt like lightening had shot through my legs, strengthening them. Something lifted me to my feet. On that fateful day, God showed up and restored my health. I am so thankful to Him for His miraculous power and His mercy toward me and millions of others.

After my healing, I rejoiced for a season. I visited my mother on the island of Jamaica and my siblings. I loved to finally be around my family. The welcome was overwhelming; everyone took time out to see me and love me. I thanked God that His love never leaves us.

When I returned to the United States, however, I started feeling depressed. Maybe I was just missing my family, I thought. The feeling of loneliness plagued me constantly and I would get emotional for no reason. I felt a longing to always be in my mother's presence. Suddenly, something was triggered in my mind, as if a volcano had erupted inside me. I started hearing nothing but negativity over and over in my head, words like, "You are not good enough," "You will never make it," and "You are a failure, and you will never succeed." On and off, I would hear voices telling me to kill myself.

By this time, I was in a supervisory role at a new job, managing others and very good at what I did. But outside those four walls, I was a husk, waiting to be blown away. I looked like I had it all—the career, the house, the education—but inside, I was empty. I suddenly didn't feel like I had enough and that I hadn't accomplished enough. I even lost interest in the Word of God because I felt that not even God understood me anymore. I wore permanent makeup that no one could see through, while underneath was a frail girl who was healed physically but was mentally like a train on the verge of derailing. I once tried to take a whole bottle of pills to end the pain. The enemy used this negativity to play a game in my head without any other players aside from him. He knew the things I liked and where I wanted to be and because I didn't understand his tactics, he taunted me and created chaos around me.

Every day, I went into the office, did an excellent job and even counseled others on their personal issues, not letting anyone in on the secret that I needed help myself. Sometimes, it felt like my mind was a ticking time bomb. I couldn't sleep. Some nights, I would lie on the bathroom floor, weeping. Finally, one night, I went to the kitchen, picked up one of the knives and went back to the bathroom. I looked at myself in the mirror and said, "It was nice knowing you, but now I must say goodbye." I put the knife to my wrist. As I drew the first blood, I heard a voice say, *"You are wonderfully and fearfully made. I love you."*

Voice crackling, I asked, "Who are you?"

He answered, "I am Jesus! I have come to save you."

In that moment, I felt like someone stopped my hand and took the knife from me. I couldn't speak as the tears ran down my cheeks. An inner peace engulfed me and it felt like I was cuddled in a blanket.

God delivered me from my infirmity and restored me to good health. He took away my brokenness and made me whole again. He set me free from my web of suicide and poured His Spirit onto me. Now, I serve Him wholeheartedly with all of my being. It's been twelve years since I received my complete healing and deliverance. I never knew that God would choose me to be a messenger of hope to His people, but I guess we don't always know where God is taking us as we journey in life. He has entrusted me to watch over others through the ministry I lead and I am humbled at the grace He has shown me. Going through this pain, heartache and ultimate healing, has shown me so much about myself and what the power of God can do. Whatever you may be going through right now, you *can* overcome.

1. I encourage you to have a foundation that is built in God. To make prayer your strong tower. Having a solid prayer life and staying in the Word of God will be like medicine to your bones and bring healing to your pain and severed heart.

2. Avoid being in the company of negative people and shun the appearance of evil. In doing so, your path will become prosperous, not only financially, but also in your health and your soul. Hurting people have a tendency to hurt others if they are not thoroughly healed. Allow God to be your Source for healing mentally, physically and spiritually. With that being said, seek medical help when necessary, but be reminded that God is the Ultimate Source of all things. Put your trust in Him in all things.

Trusting God is the key to attaining anything that you seek; His grace will show up and cover you.

Stacy

About Stacy

As a motivational speaker, author and evangelist, Stacy Y. Whyte is known as a voice of inspiration that is bringing hope to the hopeless through the Word of God and by outreach programs. She not only encourages others to walk with integrity, but empowers them to walk with a spirit of expectancy. Wherever she goes, the message of love and hope is shared among people from all social classes, and barriers are torn down. Stacy empowers others to reach their full potential and step forward into the things that God has already prepared for them. With an unshakeable faith, she continues to be a highly skilled motivator who reaches nations with her writings and teachings. She's been featured in *Caribbean Voice News, Truth in the News Magazine, Ebony News, Street Hype News Magazine* and also appeared as a guest on TBN.

To learn more, visit
www.StacyYWhyte.com

13

PATRICE TARTT

Dining At The Table of Deceit

An only child, spoiled to the core, extremely obedient, resilient and a go-getter since childhood are a few adjectives that I use to describe who I am. As a daddy's girl, my father was the apple of my eye, my heart. Losing him within a matter of three months on April 2, 2011 unexpectedly, going through the aftermath of a traumatic situation after his death, along with dealing with family drama and pain are what helped me develop into the even stronger individual I am today. I know that what doesn't kill you makes you stronger and, as cliché as this may sound, it's nothing but the truth—the whole truth at that.

I'm sure you've heard the phrase "the white elephant in the room." Oftentimes, we pretend it doesn't exist and ignore it because we're too embarrassed of it or ashamed to talk about it. It may even be considered taboo. My white elephant in the room is the betrayal, lies, and deception surrounding the death of my father. It was served to me by individuals I loved and trusted up until the day of my beloved father's funeral.

These individuals were well-prepared to present this dinner of deceit. I was underprepared to take on what they were dishing out because I was unaware it was being planned. It was, however, the last meal of its kind because I had a *divine awakening*, an epiphany to my purpose in life. This final meal was so well-planned that the red carpet was rolled out, the whitest of white table clothes was placed on the table, and the finest of fine china was set before me. *You see, your enemies will set you up as though they're doing things in your favor when, in fact, it's merely a distraction.* They'll stop at nothing until the wool has been pulled over your eyes and, little do you know, they're wolves in sheep's clothing. The white elephant in the room of betrayal from loved ones and friends exists among many people, but most of the time, they choose to ignore it.

Over the past few years, I experienced the death of two very influential, close and loving people in my life back to back. On May 2, 2010, I lost my maternal grandmother. Shortly after I returned from my grandmother's funeral, I learned I was expecting the greatest gift of my entire life. A week after giving birth to my son and being released from the hospital, I received a phone call that my father had been rushed to the hospital and then hospitalized. WOW! How could this be? Everything was fine with his health up until that point, as far as I knew. I was completely caught off guard. Adjusting to motherhood and then having to deal with the fact that my dad was in the hospital was more than I thought I could handle. However, even with this bad news, my understanding was that God wouldn't place more on you than you could bear. I was in for a rude awakening that would change my life forever. My father's health wasn't looking good at all. The doctors said that had he not made it to the ER when he did, he would have died. After delivering my son, I started having complications with my health, too. My blood pressure sky rocketed and stayed that way for weeks. I had to be placed on medication and, to make matters worse, I ended up in the ER myself due to other health complications. I remember doctors rushing into the room, telling me my blood pressure was so high and my heart was beating so fast, I was on the verge of a heart attack. Scary, right? At the same time, my father's condition was worsening. I was faced with making the decision of getting on a plane and traveling to see him only three weeks after giving birth.

Two trips later, visiting my father in ICU in Milwaukee, Wisconsin, I watched him lay on his deathbed. I felt as though my life had been placed in a shredder and torn into a million different pieces. My father would never get the opportunity to hear the words Grandpop. He would never get the chance to meet his one and only grandchild, who resembles him so heavily that, even now, people comment on how much my son looks like my father. What a traumatic experience: giving birth to a baby, leaving your three-week-old newborn to fly to your hometown to check on your parent who is suddenly diagnosed with congestive heart failure and a disease no one I knew had ever heard of.

On April 2, 2011, I felt as if someone had knocked the wind out of me; the death of my father was surreal. To this day, it's hard to believe he's gone. The day before his funeral is one I'll never forget. After returning to Milwaukee, I contacted my father's bank and was informed he only had a few hundred dollars in his account. I knew this was outlandish because, of course, my dad had more money than that. I didn't know the amount because I never inquired. His money was never my concern. He and his health were all I worried about. He was retired and everything he had was paid for, including his cars and his home.

This is when I acknowledged my white elephant in the room and the day I realized that the "last dinner" prepared for me was simply a way to keep me distracted and focused on the wrong things. It was all a façade. I hung up the phone in shock and I began to scream and cry frantically because I already knew what happened and who was responsible. How could this have happened? My father had a will and I was named the beneficiary. He was leaving everything to me except for one item, a piece of furniture in his home. There were executors named on the living will to see to it that I received everything he left for me. In addition to this, I was named beneficiary on the accounts at his bank. My next question was, "Why did God choose me and my father to endure this type of betrayal?"

As for me, the answer is simple: because *He knew I could handle it. He knew my tragedy would one day be my triumph.* Hence, my story! He knew that this child of God would be able to take that test and allow it to be my testimony. Here I was with a newborn baby, fatherless, stripped of the money, and missing valuable items from his house that were taken. What was I to do but pray? How did these individuals get away with this when a will was in place and with me being listed as beneficiary on the accounts? I've learned not to question God anymore. I know that our individual book of life is already written and it's on us to live a life that is of God and integrity.

Toni Morrison once said, "If there's a book that you want to read, but it hasn't been written yet, then *you* must write it." This is one of my favorite quotes because I feel everyone has a story within them waiting to be told. My advice to you is to write your story!

One of my many purposes in life is to share my story and to educate others so they can prevent the same thing from happening. To give strategies on how to cope with the loss of a parent or loved one while appropriately protecting yourself and others you love dearly from being betrayed, lied to and deceived. If you've experienced this personally, I want to share some words of wisdom with you so you're able to cope with this type of pain. If you haven't dealt with this type of situation, I want to share what I've learned to help *protect you* from having to endure this type of pain and heartache because, truth be told, it hurts. It's going on three years since this happened to me and it still hurts the same, but God has given me *peace that surpasses all understanding*. That's the only reason I'm able to move forward and still stand.

Patrice's P.O.W.E.R. Planning Advice:
The advice I'm sharing below is to give you VIP (Very Important Planning) tips and words of encouragement so you don't go through the same situation I did. Please note that I'm not a licensed attorney. This advice is solely based on my personal experience.

"P" **Preparing with prayer** - Prayerful preparation is key. If you leave God out of your plans, trust me, you'll have mess. We must proceed with caution and prepare with prayer. Leaving God out of our intentions is like getting into your car and driving blindfolded. Your car must have a driver, an efficient guide in order to properly operate. Let God be your driver and guide your life.

⇨ **VIP TIP**: **Prepare (with prayer) a will.** *A trust and estates attorney can assist you with this.* Also, plan long-term care (with prayer). This is advisable and important in the event something happens unexpectedly, such as an illness or injury. Five Wishes is a document you can fill out to make well-informed decisions if an accident or sickness occurs. Go to www.AgingWithDignity.org, highlight the "Five Wishes" tab and scroll down to "Fish Wishes Resources" to get more information.

Finally, be mindful of any health concerns or issues before it's too late. Be aware of rare diseases such as Amyloidosis, which I'm an advocate for. The warning signs can oftentimes be subtle. Knowledge is power!

"O" **Overcome your obstacles.** God built us with the ability to overcome all obstacles. We should be grateful he has equipped us to do this through His grace and mercy. Ultimately, you'll look back at your obstacle and define it as weak because the stronger one always prevails. That is YOU! Never let your challenges defeat you.

"W" **Winning wisely by weathering the storm.** Fight fair and win wisely. Don't allow your trials and tribulations to discourage you into giving up. WIN! Your test should be your testimony; allow yourself to go from tragedy to triumph by weathering the storm.

⇨ **VIP TIP**: Winning wisely also includes *creating a Power of Attorney* and choosing someone you can trust to act on your behalf with regard to your estate, bank accounts, etc. This goes for the executor as well. Choosing an individual who you know will handle their fiduciary duties is a smart decision.

"E" Executing excellence. Be excellent in all you execute and leave a legacy of excellence. Never allow yourself to act out of character because, at that moment, you're allowing life to get the best of you. Tell that curve ball life is trying to throw at you to stand down because you'll be better after your trial than you were before.

"R" Responsibility without regression. Be responsible and resilient. After something bad happens, you should not regress by returning to that same place you came from. Remember, we must WIN.

Through this journey, I've learned a couple of things:

1) Never give up, no matter what you're going through.

2) Stay encouraged and pray.

As women, we can handle a lot more than we give ourselves credit for. To remind you of this, I want you to try this exercise:

Look in a mirror and tell yourself, *"I am fearfully and wonderfully made; I am a child of the highest God. No weapon formed against me shall ever prosper. When I feel weak, I will ask for strength and courage; I may not trust myself, but I trust in the highest God. I don't give myself credit for all that I have already overcome, and I need to start doing so. I am powerful and I am loved. I am a warrior and I am built to OVERCOME."*

All I've been through—the ultimate extent of betrayal—hasn't been easy. However, overcoming these things has allowed me to continue in this journey called life. I am here and **I am STILL STANDING!**

Patrice

About Patrice

Patrice Tartt, is a Milwaukee, Wisconsin native, a hybrid of resiliency and passion topped off with cherry-on-top ambition. After dealing with the unexpected death of her father in 2011, Patrice was led to seek therapy through writing. Unknowingly, Patrice's therapeutic writing sessions led to the completion of her debut novel, **Wounds of Deception**, which allowed her to tell a tangled story of hurt, anger and confusion while also healing. She has a desire to educate and entertain through her writing, discussing seldom talked about topics like family betrayal, health issues, and the aftermath of pain with a creative twist. Patrice currently resides in the Washington, D.C. metro area with her young son and is an active member of Alpha Kappa Alpha Sorority, Incorporated.

To learn more, visit
www.PatriceTartt.com

14

CHERYL A. PULLINS

How To Turn a Setback into a Radical Comeback!

When I was a little girl, I was like most other little girls. I wanted to get married and had been planning my fairy tale wedding long before I was thinking about who I wanted to be when I grew up.

I had a few boyfriends. One my mom liked, but his mother didn't like me. One I really liked, but my mom didn't care for at all. There was another one who was in college in Tennessee. He was okay, but the distance helped to fizzle out that relationship. Oh yeah, there was also the one down the street who played drums at church. I have no idea what happened there.

Then there was him, "the one."

I met him the night before he left for college. His family was giving him a going away dinner, and one of his five sisters invited me to attend. Even though I didn't know him at all, his sister was one of the coolest and most stylish women I knew, so I went.

There was lots of food, people and tons of fun. When it came time for things to come to an end, he and a couple of other people walked me home. It was no biggie. The night came to a close, and that was that.

A few weeks later, his sister asked if I would write him at college. He was missing home, and she thought it would be a good idea for people to send him letters. I agreed, but since I had only met him once, I had to remind him who I was and how we met.

That one letter was the nucleus of a six-year relationship, a 14-year marriage, and two amazing daughters. As beautiful as that all may sound, it also contributed to one of the most challenging periods of my life. From the day I found photos of him with another woman hanging out together while we were engaged until the day I walked out of the marriage the second time. I lived a life full of mental and emotional abuse.

The interesting thing is that my former husband was no "ordinary" guy. He was a minister who became a pastor five months after we were married. Yes, I was a first lady during most of the marriage. I have so many different stories I could share with you about the challenges of our marriage. There was more infidelity than I care to emotionally drag you through, but I'll tell you about the day I left the marriage for the second and last time.

It was three days before my birthday and I had already told my husband I was leaving. At this point, we were sleeping in separate rooms. This night, things got out of hand. Even though there were a few types of abuse present, physical abuse was never one of them.

My boxes were packed. We were both fully aware that I was leaving. Even my daughters had been told, but on this night, a discussion about me leaving escalated, which lead to me striking him in the mouth with a phone and running out of the house to find safety at the nearby police station.

That night, I left with one dress and my purse.

It was only the beginning to a bigger setback. I was on a spiral to losing myself and my purpose for being on earth. Blinded by fear, feeling abandoned and disconnected from a sense of family and belonging, it got worse before it got better.

Getting worse culminated within a three-day stay on the mental floor of a hospital in Pennsylvania. I had bottomed out. Here I was, a mother to two amazing girls and a human resources professional for a five-billion dollar publicly traded company, sitting in a place she had never imagined in her wildest dreams. That experience was both the setting of one day and the dawn of a new one.

Because of all the anxiety in my life, I hadn't been sleeping well. So my first day there, all I wanted to do was sleep. By the second day, I was fully present and aware of my surroundings. I didn't like where I had landed, but a shift took place.

There was a woman who worked at the hospital I had not seen the day before. She took me into the family meeting room to talk to me. The first thing she said was not to take any of the pills. Her exact words to me were, *"You don't need them. You just need someone to talk to."*

She was right. I'd gone through 14 years of being in a very challenging marriage and had never told anyone what was going on. I carried it in my head and heart all those years. I had emotionally crashed and, just like computer systems that crash, I needed a reset. Even more, I needed a system cleanup. In order for me to survive, I needed to clear out all the toxic emotions and thoughts that had been plaguing me for many years. In order for me to experience a radical comeback, I had to transform my mind and heal my heart.

Many women across the globe have been increasingly experiencing challenges, which are impacting their lives in such a way they are feeling they may never recover. They're dealing with issues ranging from personal to professional, from relationships to finances, from physical to spiritual. In mass numbers, we are hearing about and seeing more and more women who are encountering bouts of depression and difficulty navigating the terrain of emotional peaks and valleys.

I wanted to share this part of my story to give you a glimpse into my journey. *How I show up in the world today is not by accident.* It was because I made an intentional choice to stage a radical comeback from my major setback.

I'm sharing because I desire the same for anyone who has found themselves off track due to life's challenges. Keep reading to discover *five things* you can do to experience the same.

How do you overcome life's adversities in order to experience a radical comeback from a major setback?

What I know is it certainly isn't easy. The number one thing you must learn is to become resilient. It's in your struggle that you find the strength to become strong. A setback is not the time for giving in or giving up. It's the time when you make a decision, create a plan, and take action.

1. See where you are going.

One of the most relied upon of the five senses is sight. On a basic level, sight is the ability to see with your physical eyes, but if you dig deeper, the ability to see includes creating a mental picture or visualization. Are you familiar with the term "mind's eye"? It refers to the human ability for visualization by experiencing visual mental imagery. Basically, it's the ability to "see" with your mind. Helen Keller said, *"The only thing worse than being blind is having sight but no vision."*

From this place of seeing, you can set yourself up for a powerful comeback. *Use your mind's eye to see yourself in the future.* Where are you? Are you living the life you dreamed of living? Are you experiencing success in all areas of your life? Are you making choices and decisions which allow you to live in freedom? Go to the mirror and say to yourself, "I see you in the future, and you look much better than you look right now!"

Visualize the life you want and deserve to live. Harness what you see to help create the path to get from where you are now to where you desire to be. Use your vision to visualize that path.

2. Pursue your passion.

Dare to craft a vision for your life. *Tap into the creativity embedded within you to reach your destined place of purpose.* Have you taken the steps necessary to connect with your purpose? That very thing you are passionate about could be the spark you need. I was inspired to help empower women because I encountered individuals who'd share with me that they didn't know or hadn't connected with their purpose, why they are on this earth at this appointed time and place. Some have stated they have no desire to invest their time, resources or energy in realizing their purpose, maximizing their potential and igniting the passion within. It is my hope that you're not at this place in your life. However, if you are, then you're reading this at the right time.

Now is the time for you to invest in you. You may have spent years, an enormous amount of resources, or endless hours working toward something that is not germane or authentic to your purpose. Take the time now to think about the thing in your life that makes you sing, the thing you talk about and people can see the twinkle in your eye and the glow in your countenance. Discover, unleash and pursue your passion.

3. Act on your goals.
Take a close look at the word "goal." The first two letters make up the word "go." *Go*, meaning to move on a course, proceed or to take a certain course. It is just that simple. Goals aren't as complicated as we make them out to be. Goals are what you want to achieve. For this example, our goal is to go food shopping. There are a number of tasks we must complete in order to reach this goal. The basic tasks include preparation, going outside, getting into the car, putting the car in gear, and going.

An effective way to help reach your goals is to break them down into a series of tasks. With this in mind, you may only want to tackle two to three goals at one time. Why? Because when you list out the tasks associated with each goal, the list can become pretty long. Begin small and be persistent and consistent in reaching your goals.

4. Rev up your engine.
In thinking about revving an engine, car racing comes to

mind. In preparation for a high speed motor race, revving the engine prepares the car for optimum performance, getting your car warmed up for the race ahead.

This is certainly a principle you can apply to your life. Revving your personal engine is a great way to prepare yourself for the race ahead. Life is often viewed as a race. It takes many components for you to not only get in the race, but to sustain it with speed, persistence, consistency and accuracy. You are the driver, and the car you have been given is called life. One of the keys to life is learning to drive and navigate with wise efficiency.

A great way to "rev up your engine" is to create positive affirmations that are consistent with the way you see your life in the future. They should be positive and written in present tense. *Remember to view your future with your mind's eye.*

5. Kick start your life!

To kick start your life is just another way to say jump start. It's time to leap into action and re-energize your life. Little to no progress can be made if you are stuck in life with no energy or passions to get the kick start you need.

I am a self-proclaimed movie aficionado. In the movie *Inception*, there was something referred to as the kick. The kick was necessary to wake up a dreaming individual to get them from one level to another. It's amazing how you can find spiritual truths in practical and natural things because sometimes, in order to get to your next level in life, you need a swift kick.

It's time to make room for new experiences by removing thoughts, ideas, negative words and even people that are not helping you get to your new level in life. What may have worked in the past may not work for your future.

Plan your comeback by connecting with the right people and changing the way you view your life in order to see it in a different way. Pursue your passion with tenacity and fervor, and get the tools and resources you need to have a powerful comeback from a setback.

Cheryl

About Cheryl

Cheryl A. Pullins, CPC was born in New York City, NY, but grew up in Philadelphia, PA, and is no stranger to challenges. She was adopted at the age of two, shot by a stray bullet at the age of nine and a former pastor's wife for fourteen years, Cheryl knows what it takes to overcome and transform lives. She started with hers first.

Known as the *Purveyor of Iconic Brands, Social Media Connoisseur and Business Mentor*, Cheryl helps women in business, who have a profound and vivid passion to serve the world with their gifts. Her passion is to strategically guide their deep reaching desire to use their imaginative business ideas as a platform to transform those ideas into iconic brands. She is a certified professional coach, a best-selling author and a frequently sought after speaker, who has received both national and international recognition for her work and commitment to working with women in the areas of life management and business.

To learn more, visit
www.iCoachWomen.com

SOLUTION – YES YOU!

A Message of Encouragement
OLIVER T. REID "The Solution Coach"

Hello, You!
Yes, I'm talking to you.

You – The Solution...

Wonderful You, Inevitable You!
You, the one with the long hair, short hair, no hair.
Yes You – the one with the dreams and visions.
The one with ideas and solutions.
The one who is fearfully and wonderfully made.
The one who they call forgotten.
You – who's been downtrodden.
You – who's been sifted and been broken beyond repair.
Yes, You!

You – who have seemed to be a distant memory in the minds of others.

You – weighing 245.
You – weighing 132.
You – who feels like nobody knows the trouble you see.

Hello, Solution!
Solution to problems that You answer in the Earth.

You – undeniable!
You – defy all the odds.
You are a solution in the Earth!

You – with no money.
You – who's mourning right now...
You – who's crying right now...

You – who's feeling sad right now...
You – who's going through it right now...
You are a solution in the Earth!

Nobody knows You.
Nobody knows your name.
But God has called *You!*

You – the victim of divorce.
You – the victim of persecution.
You – the victim, but you are a victor.
You are a solution in the Earth!

You may have been forgotten, but...
You are not bland, you are a brand plucked out of the fire.
You are a solution!

You are bigger and better than the equation.
You are undeniable and unique.
You are bigger than your YouTube.
You are bigger than your Facebook status.

***You are bigger than all of the hell that you exhaled
and been through.***

Hello You!
Wonderful You!
You are a solution because you serve *The Solution.*

God is *The Solution!*
You are a solution in the Earth!

You are full of consistent solutions—
From top to bottom, from inside and out...
YOU ARE A SOLUTION!

Oliver T. Reid

Visit Oliver at **www.I-AM-aSolution.com**

How do you feel?

What are your thoughts?

Have you found solutions to address your situation?

Are you ready to discover your purpose,
voice or true identity?

Have you discovered the courage to face your painful
tragedies, disappointments and setbacks?

Are you ready to get YOU back?

We challenge you to **Embrace The Process!**

Connect with us or share your feedback on:

www.SurvivingShockingSituations.com

Facebook.com/YouCanSurviveIt

Goodreads.com

Amazon.com

For questions or to contact one of the authors,
Send an email to Hello@PurposelyCreatedPG.com

THANK YOU FOR YOUR SUPPORT!

YOUR WRITING IS A *Sacred* GIFT.

Your words are more than an unbound
manuscript waiting to be released into
the world. It's a soon-to-be executed
divine assignment, which can
only be delivered by you.

The way it looks, feels and impacts
is a direct extension of who you were
CREATED TO BE + DESIRE TO BECOME
#TheGreatest

It's Time to Unleash Your Manuscript!

Are you ready? #PublishYourGift

CONNECT WITH US!
(866) 674-3340
Hello@PurposelyCreatedPG.com

www.PurposelyCreatedPG.com

Purposely Created
PUBLISHING GROUP

24113245R00091

Made in the USA
San Bernardino, CA
12 September 2015